The *seventeen* Guide to
KNOWING YOURSELF

THE
seventeen
GUIDE TO
KNOWING
YOURSELF

By Daniel A. Sugarman, Ph.d,
and Rolaine Hochstein

THE MACMILLAN COMPANY
NEW YORK
COLLIER-MACMILLAN LTD.
LONDON

Library of Congress Catalog Card Number: 67-18894

First Printing

THE MACMILLAN COMPANY, NEW YORK
COLLIER-MACMILLAN CANADA LTD., TORONTO, ONTARIO

Printed in the United States of America

*The facts in this book are true, but the names and
case histories have been changed to protect the
confidential relationship between psychologist
and patient.*

For Amy, Bess, Eric,
Jeremy, Kate and Rhona

Contents

Introduction

Dear Teen-ager:

The best of all reasons for learning to live with yourself is that it enables you to live happily with others—your friends, your parents, your teachers, the boys you date—without feeling pressured (or even sorely tempted) to pretend you are someone you're not. Not many of us ever achieve perfect poise and self-confidence, but the earlier we start searching for it, the more likely we are to find it.

The teen years are the best time to begin. Your childhood emotional dependence on your parents is over; for the first time you are beginning to see them as fallible people, not gods. And while much of what they have taught you about life will shape the person you will someday be, the job is by no means finished —and the rest is up to you.

What kind of adult do you want to be? It is an impossible question, isn't it? And yet you do give answers—dozens of them —in decisions you make daily: Do you face down your feelings of inferiority and shyness and try out for the lead in the class play, or settle for a backstage job? Do you date only the boys within your crowd, or venture out now and then with someone you like from another group? Do you explode with anger over a teacher's unjust accusation, or calmly explain to her why she is wrong? Do you give up your interest in physics because your father thinks it's silly for a girl, or do you pursue it in spite of him? Each of these decisions requires self-knowledge, and the girl who knows who she is obviously makes them with less agonizing and more agility than the girl who does not. The purpose of this book is to help you be one who knows.

Self-discovery is perhaps the most exciting form of exploration. A sudden insight bursts into a shower of sparks, illuminating a shadowy corner of fear or worry or doubt or anger, and you are never quite the same person again. *"That's* why I react that way!" you say, and everything is different because now you understand. Little by little, insight by insight, you learn the terrain of your own emotions—what triggers your inferiority feelings, why you daydream about your math teacher, how guilt over growing away from parents makes you feel angry with them. The more you learn about yourself, the more you grow, for psychological awareness is what fosters emotional growth.

The authors of this book understand that well; and chapter by chapter, you can look forward to an exhilarating lesson in you— the girl you are, the girl you can be.

Most sincerely,

Enid A. Haupt
Editor-in-Chief
SEVENTEEN

The *seventeen* Guide to
KNOWING YOURSELF

What It Means To Be a Girl Now

> When I have a brand-new hairdo
> With my eyelashes all in curl,
> I float as the clouds on air do,
> I enjoy being a girl!*

When everything's going right, many of you, like the singer of this song in the Broadway musical *Flower Drum Song,* really enjoy being girls. Yet recent surveys show that, while almost all boys are glad of their masculinity, a substantial number of girls would prefer to be boys. Whether you believe that ours is a man's world or not, you are going to live in this world as a woman. What this means depends upon your own definition of femininity. Before you are a woman, you are a person. But what kind of person you are grows out of your feelings about yourself as a woman.

Social scientists have discarded the idea that any particular piece of human behavior can be described as either "feminine" or "masculine." While it is true that no man has ever borne a baby, all traits beyond biological differences between men and women are acquired as we grow up. At various times and places in history, every characteristic that we now consider feminine has been considered masculine.

Too often, narrow or unquestioned ideas about femininity get in the way of a girl's development as a person. A grade-schooler who wants to set up a science laboratory in her basement is discouraged from this project and pushed instead into a ballet class by her mother, who says, "Dancing is more suitable for young ladies." A junior high school girl is left behind while her father takes her brother out for baseball practice—even though she loves to play ball. In a study of teen-agers a few years ago, one psychologist found that some girls pretended to be inferior when they were with boys, "playing dumb" and going so far as to conceal their good marks. Asked why, the girls replied that boys preferred them that way. Many a girl leaves her aptitudes undeveloped as she tries to fit herself into a stereotype of femininity.

Many parents, even today, feel that college is necessary only for their sons. Not very long ago a father of two boys and two girls told me, "I'm glad I don't have to worry about the girls' education. All they need to know is how to run a house and raise children." Aside from the narrowness of his opinion, his facts are wrong. An estimated nine in ten of today's teen-age girls will hold paying jobs at some time in their lives. Most will work before they have children and many will work again when their children are all in school. Some will work to support a husband in graduate school and others will enjoy careers of their own, whether or not they marry and have children. Even those who won't have paying jobs will probably do volunteer work of one kind or another. Very few, if any, girls growing up today will need to know nothing more than housekeeping and child-raising. But even if you turn out to be the one in ten who never holds a job outside her home, there are few challenges in life as demanding as the raising of a child to healthy maturity. This is what Dr. Charles McIver, the late president of the University of North Carolina's Woman's College, had in mind when he said, "When you educate a man, you educate an individual; when you educate a woman, you educate a whole family."

As girls you have rapidly broadening horizons, and it is time for some straight thinking about what it means to be a woman in late-twentieth-century America.

It means choices. Our society's notion of a woman's role is changing very rapidly and there is no longer just one acceptable way to be a woman. Almost every line of work is open to women and the prejudice that has held women back from career advancement is gradually giving way. While many of you will want to be at home while your children are growing, you will be able to choose—the way a man does—from many different possibilities a direction that best fits your own needs and inner drives: you can consciously work toward your goals of security, adventure, prestige, wealth, service to others or creative self-expression. If you choose a traditional way of life, it will be because you want to, not because there are no other roads open.

It means responsibility. In 1920, when women finally won the right to vote in the United States, there were strings attached; they also took on a responsibility to be informed about their government and the political, social and economic issues of their time. Similarly, when women claim the right to work, they have an obligation to be competent and conscientious. With broadening opportunities for education and self-realization, there are proportionately increasing demands. Men expect their wives to be companions as well as capable homemakers. Employers expect their female employees to meet professional standards. "I'm only a woman" is not—as it once was—an excuse for inefficiency, ignorance or failure to keep up with the world; and "She's beautiful but dumb" is hardly a compliment. Today's woman has not only the right but also the responsibility to live up to her full potential.

It means a broadening of the definition of femininity. A woman is a strong, naturally aggressive person who goes out to hunt and fight while the man, as befits his gentler nature and weaker physique, stays home to prepare food and tend the children.

Does this description seem all wrong? It may to you, but in other eras and even in some primitive societies right now, it was and is considered the way of the world.

Let's move to western civilization just over a hundred years ago, when the three Brontë sisters chose to publish their novels and poetry under masculine pen names because nice ladies simply didn't write for publication. A few years later, another English lady broke convention by opening up a hospital on a battlefield of the Crimean War. It was eccentric enough for Florence Nightingale to be a nurse—against the sensitive and delicate female nature; nursing was a man's job—but to go off to war was nothing short of madness. Today, of course, nursing is almost entirely a woman's field. But try an experiment: ask your father how he'd like to have his appendix removed by Karen Kildare, M.D.

Women doctors in the United States today usually work against a good deal of prejudice. Yet in the Soviet Union, most doctors are women, who are considered "by nature" better fitted for the profession.

Is it feminine to wear cosmetics and complicated hairdos and pretty clothes? Not in some African communities, where the men paint their faces, construct elaborate coiffures with red mud (instead of teasing and spraying) and drape themselves in colorful costumes while the women feel they have no time for such vanity.

Is it feminine to be interested in the domestic arts of cooking and knitting and needlework? Members of the Royal Air Force, one of the bravest and toughest fighting units of World War II, regularly relaxed between missions by knitting socks and sweaters and sewing patchwork quilts.

Considering just these random examples, you'll have to conclude that femininity is a relative term. A sound working definition of femininity would include characteristics that a certain society sees as belonging particularly to women. Since our society's notion of the woman's role is changing, our definition of femininity is an extremely flexible one. There are, of course, traditionalists. How often have you heard it said of a small, shy, dainty toddler: "Oh, she's a real girl"? What about her tall, sturdy, high-spirited playmate? Is she less of a girl? Elizabeth

Taylor, the world's most famous sex symbol, is neither small nor retiring. Is she not feminine?

Old-fashioned ideas of what makes a "real girl" are disappearing, however, as girls prove they can be feminine and athletic, feminine and intellectual, feminine and aggressive, feminine and independent, feminine and successful in business. Not long ago, the woman of achievement outside the home found it hard to be accepted in a "man's world." Put on the defensive, she often compensated by acting and looking as much like a "businessman" as possible. But as she became less exceptional, she was able to be more herself and was less compelled to act a role she did not really feel.

With many roads already paved for you, it's possible to work toward whatever goal you have in mind and still accept and enjoy being a girl. Instead of acting out a "woman's role," you can write your own script. By now, you should already be thinking about and preparing for your future. Some of you will find fulfillment in taking care of your family's needs, watching your children grow, running a warm and gracious household and helping your husband advance in his career. Others will find satisfaction in careers of your own. Most of you will try to enjoy the best of both worlds by combining—to the degree that suits you—families and careers. To choose a role that is suited to your individual needs, you must give considerable thought to your personal definition of femininity.

Your concept of what it means to be a girl begins to be shaped almost on the day you are born. In the hospital nursery, baby girls are wrapped in pink blankets, baby boys in blue. The fathers hover at the window and those who have girls say, "Isn't she sweet?" while the fathers of boys say, "He's some big buster!"

Society is only too eager to teach you the traditional female role. If you can remember your early childhood, you can probably recapture many occasions of hearing adults say, "Don't hit Billy. Little girls don't fight" and "Come out of that mud. Girls have to stay clean" and, of course, "Please act like a lady," which meant a lot of things, usually restrictive.

You were probably expected to play with dolls and tea sets, to want a frilly bedroom and to be interested in clothes. If you liked baseball and blue jeans, you were called a "tomboy." By the time you were seven or eight, you already had a fairly well developed notion of what was expected of a "good girl." The majority of you went along with it, helping mother in the kitchen, taking piano lessons and playing more sedentary games than your riproaring brothers.

Growing up in a home where a girl is cherished and the mother is happy about her own life is the best way for a girl to feel positive and accepting of her womanhood. If your mother enjoyed cooking and let you share her fun with it, if she taught you to sew and encouraged you to decorate your own room, you probably have good feelings about domesticity. And if your father was attentive and appreciative of your mother—and of you—you are likely to have a good feeling about men and marriage.

One reason for many girls' difficulties in accepting their femininity is that while growing up they probably had many more restrictions and fewer privileges than their brothers. Another, even more common, is that their mothers were dissatisfied with their lives.

Recently I worked with a desperately unhappy girl who, at eighteen, had never dated or shown any interest in boys. She came to my office carelessly dressed and without make-up. After talking to her about her background, I learned that she had never had a feminine model with whom she could happily identify. Her mother was a slave to housekeeping, constantly complaining of overwork and never—at least as far as her daughter could discern—having any fun. The girl was convinced that being a woman meant being a hopeless drudge. She was acting like a man—not because it was her nature, but because she was making a show of rejecting her femininity.

Other problems arise in some families where the father wanted a son "to carry on the family name." Such a father may try to make a son of his daughter or, if he has a boy too, he may favor his son. In either case, a girl has a hard time accepting her sex. In homes where the mother is absent, a girl child may be overloaded with domestic responsibility to the point where she, too, rebels against femininity.

Beyond the family itself, there are other tremendous social pressures that may reinforce, expand or twist your feelings about what it means to be a girl. Most communications media have a limited view of "feminine" interests. The women's pages of your local newspapers, for example, deal with food and fashion, decoration, gardening, clubs and social events. In a typical Hollywood movie, the romantic heroine never seriously questions her goals in life. In fact, she is usually not called upon to think at all. As either the appurtenance or the target of the romantic hero, she is a doll—in the sense of a pet or a prize. And if you think movies don't influence you, just remember the last time you tried a hairdo or posture or speech mannerism of a popular movie star.

Most television females are categorical and one-dimensional: the flippant wife, the understanding mother, the snappy career girl, the glamorous *femme fatale,* the demure western schoolteacher, the hardboiled western bar hostess and the brave widow. "Identification" is what the TV writer is asked to achieve, and if he is successful, you the viewer put yourself into the character's place, thereby getting another slant on "what it's like to be a woman."

In a week of TV commercials, you will meet an army of women whose goal in life is to make their windows sparkle, their floors shine and their wash come out whiter than their neighbor's. Each has a friend who spends *her* time making comparisons between brands. Every one is masochist enough to receive guests who visit only to catch their hostess with a stained kitchen sink, spots on her tumblers or dust in her corners. Silly as they are, these images also influence your thinking, or at least the thinking of the society that influences your thinking.

That society has an ethic and a morality that go back thousands of years to the era of Moses and the Ten Commandments. Though many ages and many philosophies have enriched our thought, a great deal of our basic way of life goes back to concepts of biblical times. To a greater or lesser degree, then, all of us are influenced by the biblical way of looking at things. Man came first; woman was his helpmate. Eve, made from Adam's rib, was subordinate and weak. Yet our highest concepts of womanly devotion—to a family and to country—also come from the Bible. The patience of a Sarah, the loyalty of a Ruth, the providence of a Rebecca have come down to us as womanly virtues. Whether consciously or unconsciously, they are probably part of your ideal.

Almost everyone, as she grows up, has a model—a teacher, a family friend, a character from history or literature, a famous contemporary, or even a friend's older sister—upon whom she tries to pattern herself. Often a girl develops a "crush" on her ego-ideal, which usually symbolizes a desire to be close to and to learn from the object of her admiration. The ego-ideal can be a powerful liberating and motivating force for girls, just as heroes tend to define and direct the ambition of boys.

Some girls will feel drawn to a soft and motherly woman, others to a fashionable sophisticate, and others to a certain teacher who, though plain in appearance, seems to be a happy, self-assured female who is accomplishing important things.

In spite of all these influences on your attitudes toward your own femininity—early experiences at home, in school, at the movies or the TV set, and with the people you meet—there is still room for free choice regarding your own, unique brand of femininity. Once you see that femininity in itself is neither good nor bad, but just there—not a goal, but a starting point—you will neither have to work at it nor rebel against it. For what you decide to do with your life is up to you. Here are ten ideas that may help you to make the most of it.

1. *Be yourself.* Like the girls who pretend to be dimwitted because they think boys will like them better that way, many of you have fallen into the habit of conforming to outside opinion (or what you *think* is outside opinion). If I had a rose for every girl who—on the day of this writing—sacrificed a dream, an opportunity or an adventurous impulse on the altar of "femininity," I'd have the biggest bouquet you ever saw.

Of course you want to be attractive to boys. But there are as many varieties of boys around as of girls. By playing up or down to a boy's idea of femininity, you're likely to attract a boy who would be great for somebody else—but not you. There is no one type of girl who has a corner on the popularity market. Be yourself—and enjoy it—and you'll have the best chance of finding someone who likes what you are.

The same holds true for planning the life you want to live. Most of us are influenced by our friends. But your friends can't make important decisions for you. If your crowd is career-minded and you want nothing more than the love of a good man and the joy of making him a happy home full of children and cooking smells and pretty things, you may end up feeling guilty about what the crowd sees as lack of ambition. But since you are the one who's going to live it, you have to suit yourself in choosing a way of life.

Being yourself also means accepting your own body. What you can't improve, you must learn to live with. Many of the things that bother you are a matter of fickle fashion. We've already seen pointed bosoms go round and, with recent styles, round bosoms go flat. Have you taken a good look at the figures that drove your great-grandfathers wild with desire? By today's fashion standards, they'd need a month at a dieters' retreat!

2. *Be self-sufficient.* While it's true that many boys enjoy dating nonaggressive, nondemanding girls, few want to associate themselves permanently with a helpless wife. Independence makes you no less feminine and a lot more desirable in today's world where women are expected to think for themselves. A self-sufficient girl is not necessarily selfish or domineering; she is simply able to make her own decisions and to contribute her opinions and preferences.

Whether you run a home, hold down a job or work out a combination, you need to be competent, efficient and resourceful. Never underestimate the skill required to manage a household or the judgment needed to bring up children. These traits don't appear magically at the ringing of wedding bells.

Such eventualities as widowhood, divorce, late marriage or none at all, or a husband who is away a good part of the year should not be shrugged off. Only the woman who has trained herself to be a whole individual can cope with these possibilities.

3. *Like men.* Liking a man and loving him are two separate feelings. I've worked with women who literally loved many men, but who didn't like any of them. Awe, fear, sexual attraction, the joy of conquest they felt; but not liking. The reasons are usually complex. A girl whose father was unloving or brutal is likely to reject or feel hostile to all men. A girl who grows up in the shadow of a clearly favored older brother frequently transfers her jealousy and rage to men in general, the old battle being fought on ever-new battlefields. A girl who was indoctrinated—perhaps by a mother who hated sex—to believe that "every boy is after only one thing" is likely to be suspicious and resentful of boys. So in many ways, despite sexual attraction, girls may have to learn to like boys.

Think over your own attitudes. Do you see boys as tin cans to be shot off a fence, one by one? Or as rungs in your ladder to status? As free tickets to places you want to go or threats to your virtue and good name? Or as a higher breed to be waited upon and bowed down to? All of these concepts of boys are damaging to the girl who holds them. Boys are persons, individuals to be taken on their own merits rather than seen through prejudices about their gender. You don't have to like all boys any more than you have to like all Swedes or all tailors—or all girls. But certainly there are many boys you should be able to respect and trust and enjoy.

Since you will probably be married, have boy-children and work with men in your future, it's crucially important to understand your feelings toward them—and to be able to like them.

4. *Enjoy being a girl.* There is really no longer any reason to resent the fact that you weren't born a man. Anything he can do, you can do—though you may have to work harder at it. In addition, you can—as no man can—enjoy the warmth and wonder of being a mother, of carrying a child in your own body and bringing him up in your own way.

There are other perquisites of being a girl in our society which you can enjoy—if you want to. Bubble baths, lacy lingerie, experimental hairdos, a stuffed bear on your bed and a frilly canopy above it are all girly fun. Other privileges of the game: having boys call *you* for dates, having them open doors for you and stand when you enter a room.

But if you enjoy the deference and gallantry of a gentleman, give your boy friend a chance to display them by remembering to be a lady. You can't expect a boy to open a door for you if you've pushed him out of the way in order to get there first.

5. *Develop interests.* If you marry a rich, fatherly man, you might just get by in life by merely looking pretty, being agreeable and loving your family. But who wants just to "get by" when she has a chance really to "get in"?

First off, most men want wives who can understand what they're talking about and can contribute to their thinking. Most men prefer companionship to adornment and want interesting as well as interested wives. What makes you interesting are your own interests, cultivated and enjoyed and talked about.

Second, the most solidly constructed life plan *can* come apart at the seams. You may find yourself—quite unexpectedly—looking for a job someday. Without skills, background or interests, what more can you hope to find than a routine, menial stopgap?

Finally, you may find—as many of your mothers have—that home life becomes less satisfying when your youngest child is in school and that you want other outlets. If you have a few deep interests, it will be easier for you to find constructive and rewarding pursuits.

For practical reasons, then, as well as for the enrichment they bring, it's important to have hobbies or areas of study. A passion for baroque music or American history, delight in needlework or ceramics make you more of a person, and a person who is more valuable to society. To quit school or drop career plans because you plan to marry is almost always a mistake; too many women who did now seek remedies in psychologists' offices.

6. *Remember your obligations.* To many women, it sometimes seems as if they have no choices because whenever they look at the clock, it's time for them to fulfill another obligation. The trick is to take on only those you can comfortably fulfill.

A young woman once consulted me because she felt distressed

with the responsibilities that fell upon her with the birth of her first child. Describing her situation to me, she commented, "After all, I got married to *escape* responsibility."

Of all the things marriage isn't, it most emphatically isn't an escape. When you take on a husband, you owe him not only love and loyalty but also a warm and comfortable home, interest in his work, sympathy for his problems, companionship in his pleasures. When you have children, you owe them the best up-bringing you can give them in addition to unflagging devotion. Any woman who makes light of these obligations is failing to fulfill a debt, and if you won't want them, you had better stay single until you do.

7. *Prepare for marriage*. ". . . and then they were married and lived happily ever after" is the end to a fairy tale, but marriage is only the beginning of a real-life story. A good relationship between two people is built brick by brick, not prefabricated. And it should have a solid foundation.

Sentiment has it that as long as two people are truly in love with each other, everything will work out fine. Almost every girl on her wedding day thinks she is in love with the man she marries; our high and rising divorce statistics indicate that this is far from enough.

The fate of a marriage depends largely upon the wife. In our culture, women are the traditional carriers of the burden of human relationships and usually concentrate more than their husbands on home and family matters. Before you join a man's life, work out your problems of selfishness and jealousy. Be sure you are generous and yielding enough to become half a couple. Select a man who is ready himself to begin the marital adventure, who can make decisions and face responsibilities.

And there are practical skills to learn. While more schools are conducting marriage and family courses, there are still girls who come to marriage trained only in secretarial skills or liberal arts. But knowing how to cook, budget and keep a house orderly and even knowing the facts of sex are all too often absent from a bride's dowry.

8. *Don't feel that you must marry.* By the time you're twenty or twenty-two, the crowd begins to change into a group of young married couples. The girls who are left start feeling pressure to "settle down." Their parents inquire about current boys with heightened interest. Their relatives may be bold enough to ask what's the matter. And their married friends will be forever fetching up bachelors for introductions.

Sometimes these pressures force a girl into premature marriage. Often they make her feel either anxious or ashamed of her single status. But spinster is not a dirty word—any more than bachelor is. A girl has the right not to marry and should be able to stay single without feeling like an oddity or a reject.

A spinster can live as meaningfully, happily and productively as a married woman. Certainly she is better off than a woman caught in a lonely or abrasive marriage. There are good reasons for choosing to remain single, among them an unwillingness to take on family responsibilities, a single-minded dedication to art or service, a reluctance to "settle down," or simply not finding a man you want to marry.

All of these conditions may change as you grow older. And if you wait until you have resolved them, your chances of a happy marriage will multiply. Statistics consistently show that the older you are when you marry, the likelier your marital happiness.

9. *Be a person before becoming a wife.* Self-sufficiency, emotional maturity, enjoyment of men, cultivated interests, knowledge of basic household skills go a long way toward making a whole woman—and a fine wife.

Sexual attraction and dating fun may be enough to make some men propose marriage. But the first flush of young love by itself is not enough to hold a marriage together.

A few weeks ago, I saw a woman of twenty-five whose prettiness was almost erased by anxiety and fatigue. Married at eighteen, she now had four children and her husband was having a blatant affair with another woman. What had happened was that he had outgrown her. She wasn't much more than a child when they were married and she hadn't had a chance—what with children and housekeeping duties—to develop her own potentials. Her husband was rising in the business world. He had little to talk about with her and was embarrassed to take her out among his associates. Boredom and discontent made him ripe pickings for a lady executive with a penchant for other women's husbands.

This is not an unfamiliar story. Whether or not they have careers of their own, women today have to keep up with their husbands. Men expect a lot of their wives, including good sense, companionship and shared interests. As an ambitious man grows in his career, he can easily leave a wife behind—intellectually and socially.

The best way to avoid this pattern is by becoming a full-fledged person, woman enough to hold a man's interest.

10. *Write your own ending to your life story.* Though it sometimes doesn't seem so, you actually have a great deal of control over your life. There are many circumstances you can't change, but there are even more that you can. If your parents don't want to send you to college, you can get a tuition loan and work for your board. If you want a career, you can break your crowd's precedent and start one. If the pressures of your community seem to be pushing you against a wall, you can move out. No girl today has to follow a script that's handed to her. There is nothing unfeminine about following your own special star.

In the fairy tale, Cinderella married Prince Charming. But what happened next? Did she help him run his kingdom? Did she go to graduate school and become a teacher? Did she have child after child to keep her from facing the question of what to do with herself? Or was she terribly, terribly bored?

Nobody knows the sequel to the fairy tale. Maybe it's better that way; the follow-up can be whatever each of us wants, just as *your* future is a challenge to your own imagination.

The Pleasures and Problems of Friendship

Loneliness is one of the most common teen-age problems. Almost everyone knows that you can feel lonely in a crowd: it's not a question of the presence of people, but of your involvement with them. An attractive college sophomore named Judy came to my office recently.

"I'm surrounded by people all day," she lamented, "in class, at the dining hall, in my dormitory. I get lots of phone calls, have plenty of dates and I'm even a class officer. Yet I'm lonely."

When I had talked for a while with Judy, it became clear to both of us that with all her popularity, she didn't have a single real friend. Actually, her popularity had *prevented* the development of close friendships. It was only after she chose to narrow her social circle that she began to experience the sharing of friendship and not to feel lonely anymore.

As Judy's experience shows, popularity has very little to do with friendship. That precious gift is open to anyone who really wants to have a friend and is truly willing to *be* a friend. But it is not easy. Friendship has to be worked at. When the girl who is lucky enough to be "in demand" allows herself to flit from person to person, from party to party, she can't possibly give much time and attention to any one friend. This doesn't mean that popularity or group participation isn't good, but most of us need to work out a balance between group and individual friendships.

Think for a moment of all the people you know. You'll probably find that many are acquaintances, boys and girls you know well enough to say hello to and exchange a few words with as you meet between classes or at the soda fountain. A smaller number will fall into the category of your "clique" or "crowd"—boys and girls you occasionally double-date with; perhaps they've worked with you on a class project or are members of your club. You know them better than your acquaintances, but not so well as your "companions" with whom you spend more time individually. A companion is someone with whom you do things: you may have one companion for bowling, another for homework, another for folk music concerts. Many girls, for many reasons, never get beyond companion relationships. But friendship goes deeper.

The close friend is a confidante. She is probably also a companion because she shares many interests with you. But, while mere companionship is limited to the bowling lanes, the concert hall or the study rooms, friendship goes beyond the activities at hand. A friend is sympathetically interested in the things you do that don't include her. She admires you, enjoys you, accepts your faults along with your virtues and wants to help you achieve your goals. She trusts you with her confidences and is responsive to yours. It's the confidante or close friend of whom you say, "She's just like a sister to me."

During the teen years, girls tend to move from category to category. A companion becomes a confidante perhaps after just a few get-togethers. A close friend leaves for an out-of-town college and gradually recedes into the background of your life. There will be some roller-coaster rides from acquaintance to close friend and back again, all a natural byproduct of a teen-ager's growing and testing. You should, however, be able to enjoy all levels of friendship; a companion or an acquaintance does not necessarily *have* to become a confidante, every friend need *not* be "like a sister." Some will be closer than others and there is no reason to demand a closeness from every girl you like. On the other hand, it is important to remember that while some friend-ships "just happen," others have to be made to happen. And always, they have to be helped along.

Choosing your friends. Many girls have problem friendships because they choose the wrong friends. Do you ever single out a girl because she has lots of dates and can probably give your own social life a boost? Do you go out of your way to make a friend in a higher status group than yours? Do you latch on to a "brain," hoping she'll help you pull through some of your weak subjects? How about the girl with her own car or a marvelous wardrobe in your size? Many friends are chosen for their *usiful-ness,* but few such friendships can withstand the tests of time and loyalty.

On the other side of the fence are girls who select friends to whom they can feel superior. A need to outdo or to dominate often causes girls to form master-slave relationships. Others habi-tually take up with girls of whom their parents or their crowd dis-approve. Is wishy-washy Dina your friend because you enjoy her company or because she's easy to boss around? Is tough, over-flirtatious Nan your buddy because you two have a lot in common or because you like to shock people by associating with her? If you're forever dissatisfied with the way your friendships work out, you probably should look into your reasons for choosing your friends. Some sound bases for working friendships are:

Compatibility: A friend's disposition should harmonize with your own. For example, people who like to live by a tight schedule seldom respond to those who go in for impromptu visits and unplanned outings. Sedate girls are often put off by bouncier personalities. While it's true that opposites sometimes attract, there must be understanding and appreciation on each side to prevent collision. Think: are you compatible with all your friends?

Mutual interests: Naturally, you should have friends who have attitudes and ideas in common with you. Your closest friends ought to be girls who share many of your deepest interests. But I must emphasize the value of having some friends who think and act differently from you: this is one way to grow, to develop understanding.

Proximity: If you are in New York and your best friend lives in California, you're missing something. Of course, you write letters and you may get to see her during vacations, but you ought to have a friend closer than a continent away. Part of friendship is getting together often, talking things over and having fun together. Making friends with the girl next door is a more promising venture than trying to hold first place on your list for someone who is far away.

Admiration: There is a big difference between choosing a

friend because you admire her and cultivating someone because you admire something she has—be it popularity or lovely clothes. The former is an honest offering of friendship; the latter is social climbing. Mutual admiration is a good basis for friendship.

Breaking the ice. When we talk about choosing friends, we must also consider how to meet appropriate prospects. Choice doesn't mean much to the girl who has trouble meeting people. Having worked with girls who never get beyond the acquaintance stage of friendship, I have found most of them to be shy and very much wrapped up in themselves. Timidity and self-absorption often, but not always, go together. The best way to combat this common kind of shyness is, of course, to become interested in other people, thereby forgetting yourself. Almost all of you, however, can benefit from using the six "ice-breakers" I recommend to shy girls:

1. *Say hello first.* Being the first to say hello shows that you like people and are willing to accept them in an open, friendly manner. Make it your practice always to greet a familiar face with a smile and a cheerful salutation. You may be surprised at the number and the warmth of the responses you get.

2. *Work out your feelings of rejection.* All of us have some fear of being rejected by others. It helps to remember that most other people feel just as you do and that even those with brave façades are probably afraid that *you* won't like *them.* When you try to make the other person feel comfortable, you tend to forget your own doubts. Remember also that nobody is accepted by

everyone. So if it's your turn to be rejected despite your efforts to be friendly, take it philosophically. Try again with the next girl. Besides, friendliness is habit-forming; every attempt is good practice.

3. *Join a club or a special interest group.* The most interesting people in the world are those who are interested. Whether you are interested in Richard Chamberlain, fashion, tennis or stamp-collecting, there are bound to be people who share that interest. One way to find friends is to join a group devoted to that interest —a political group, a fan club, a class in fashion design, a stamp club. There are also service groups and church fellowships where you can meet people your own age.

It's not easy for most people to join a group "cold." But if you're new in town or have no friend already in the group to prepare the way for you, then the first step is up to you. As long as a group is open to the public, you can assume that it wants you as much as you want to join. Most such groups, in fact, are eager for new members. So exercise your backbone and go down there and join.

4. *Try to help the new girl.* If you've felt friendless, you're in a good position to understand the loneliness of a new transfer student in your school or the girl who just moved in across the street. Welcome her. Offer to show her around. Introduce her (and maybe yourself, while you're at it). Perhaps you can join a local teen-age group together. In helping someone else, you may lose some of your own shyness as well as make a friend.

5. *Volunteer and invite.* To a girl bemoaning her lack of invitations, I put the question: "When was the last time *you* gave a party?" The answer was that though she had helped other girls give parties, she had never given one of her own. I told her to get stepping.

Nothing prevents you from taking the initiative and inviting people to your house. Even if one of them can't make it, she ought to be flattered that you asked her. I know there are snobs and meanies around, but I've really never met anyone who was insulted at getting an invitation. Choose your guests from those of your acquaintances who seem to have the most potential for friendship with you. At the very least, they'll know that you would like to know them better.

Likewise, you are free to volunteer for school jobs. There is always a call for help on the yearbook or a dance decoration committee. Step up when the call goes out.

6. *Be a friend to yourself.* People who feel left out of things often become their own worst enemy. They mope or sulk and punish themselves by staying home and avoiding all activities. Yet it is just at these times—when you're feeling friendless—that you need your own friendship. Take yourself out shopping, skating, to a movie or a museum. Find a hobby, a part-time job, volunteer to help at the local hospital. Go so far as to attend a stag dance alone. Dismal? Maybe. But maybe not. It's certainly not so dismal as withdrawing into a cocoon of self-pity. Besides, by keeping busy and getting out, you might meet some interesting people.

Developing friendships. Between meeting people and forming close friendships, there is a bridge that is very short for some and almost impossibly long for others. Some girls continually make acquaintances which never ripen into friendship. Usually, it's because they haven't learned the techniques of moving from the casual end of the friendship scale toward a deeper involvement. Even when these girls seem to have made a real friend, the relationship doesn't last and is at best a stormy one.

There is a pattern to these troublesome friendships; the trouble can often be traced to one girl's simply not caring enough to submerge her own convenience or desires in favor of her friend's. You girls call it selfishness, arrogance, self-centeredness or conceit; but it boils down to this: a girl who puts her own interests first at all times is not a good friend and is therefore unlikely to have good friends. A girl who considers her friend's welfare, not more than but as much as her own, will be loyal and honest and tolerant. She won't balk at putting herself out to do a favor for a friend. Friendship implies responsibility. If you go on summer vacation and don't write, you may return to find yourself minus a friend, just as you will if you keep breaking dates with her because something better turns up.

Loyalty is essential to friendship. It's easy for most people to keep confidences, but there are more severe tests. Say that a club you've wanted to join—an exclusive friendship club—decides to accept you and not your friend. Would you refuse to join without her? A loyal girl would refuse to join a group that discriminated against her friend. If you had a special friend whom the girls in your crowd disliked, would you be loyal enough to stick up for her? Could you close off their criticism with, "I know you don't like Sally, but I value her friendship"? With tact and honesty, it's possible to maintain your friendship with Sally and your crowd. The group will often respect you more for your strong stand; it sometimes learns to accept Sally, too. Actually, it's a good idea to have friends outside your crowd; it makes you a broader person.

Let's change sides now and turn you into Sally. How do you, as Sally, react to a friend's belonging to a crowd in which you are either not interested or not accepted? Are you too possessive to allow your friend to have interests apart from yours? Jealousy and resentment of outside interests and other friendships cause a great deal of trouble between girls. Yet a one-and-only relationship isn't good for anyone; the world is too large to limit your relationships to a single alter ego (or other self). It's almost like being best friends with your mirror reflection. Sooner or later the alter ego is going to insist upon *her* right to be an individual, which is indeed everyone's right. Tolerance, then, of your friend's rights to other friends and interests, of her tastes and ideas that don't match yours, is an essential quality of friendship.

Everyone is imperfect. When you can't accept a friend's imperfections and look past them toward more positive qualities, you can't be real friends. You are not your friend's teacher or psychologist, her fashion consultant or social director. You cannot make her over into your own image. Friendship implies acceptance of a person *as she is.* If you aren't able to work out a way of living with your own and other people's faults, you might as well save up for a one-way trip to Robinson Crusoeville.

The necessity of honesty in friendship seems to me to need little explanation. Of course you are truthful with your friend. But truth can be a hurtful weapon if it is used without tact. There's no need to tell Sally what some other girl said about her —unless, of course, it was something complimentary. Being honest doesn't mean you must repeat everything you hear. If a great date should pop up for an evening when you had a casual appointment with Sally, be honest enough to tell her and ask if you could postpone your appointment. If Sally asked your opinion on a dress she was about to buy, I'm sure you would try to steer her away from an unflattering line and toward a becoming style. Friendships can't operate on any basis but an honest one.

Finally, in developing friendships, you might think about what you bring to a friend. Responsibility, loyalty, tolerance and honesty are the staples; but there is another, varying quality which I'll call flexibility. Are you game? Are you ready to go out and do things with your friends? If you're sports-minded, do you refuse to do anything unathletic—go to a play, join in a hootenanny— which your friend might enjoy? Aside from your own interests, are you willing to share or at least experiment with some of hers? Give and take is what makes friendship work. Good friends are neither tyrants nor doormats; they strike a balance.

Keeping friends. Even in the most flourishing friendship, problems arise. When they do, the friendship is threatened. If the problems are handled wisely, the friendship may actually be strengthened. The key to working out problems is good communication. Don't bury your resentment, anger or disappointment, but tell your friend calmly: "This is the way I feel. . . ." A direct approach, without scolding or sarcasm, opens the door to a reasonable exchange of opinions, explanations and perhaps apologies.

Sometimes, by her actions, a girl reveals herself to be incapable of the kind of friendship you had hoped to form. But she may still be a fine bowling partner. Accept her, then, as a companion and don't ask for something that she cannot give.

In keeping friends for a long time, we almost always come up against the problem of jealousy. Time brings changes: Ginny's family moves to a grand new house; Rhoda gets pinned to a college boy; Betty is awarded a scholarship to art school; Jennifer goes to Europe for the summer. Jealousy is not unnatural, but it would be easier to fight if it weren't such a master at camouflage. If you find yourself newly critical of your friend, if you hear yourself gossiping about her, if you keep coming out with "good-natured" needling comments, watch out. Look beneath your words and actions to see if jealousy isn't at the root of them.

A pang of envy at a friend's good fortune is no cause for alarm. The best thing to do is to mention it and forget about it. But persistent, deep jealousy is different. If you feel deeply jealous, take stock of yourself. Maybe you should be working to get what your friend has instead of using up your energy in feeling jealous. Does she have so many more boy friends than you? Maybe you'd better work on your appearance and personality. And then you might ask her to arrange a blind date for you.

It also helps to look at your friend's prizes objectively. She may have moved to a lovely new house, but would you like to have her grouchy father? She worked very hard for that scholarship; would you be willing to put in that much time over your school-books? Don't be swayed by appearances. Nobody has all the cookies in the bakery.

Perhaps the hardest blow to a friendship occurs when one girl finds a boy friend she really likes and the other does not. When your friend is dating, she can't spend as much time with you as before. Also, she may no longer want to give you the blow-by-blow descriptions you shared after more casual dates. You don't have to take a back seat for your girl friend's boy friend, but you will do well to take a side seat gracefully. If you are dating too, double dates can be the answer. Wouldn't it be lovely if all your girl friends and all your boy friends liked one another?

Often a boy you are dating resents, of all people, your closest girl friend. No surprise: he would rather have you all to himself. But don't make the mistake of giving up a friend to please a boy friend. You can arrange to see her when he's not around. In the long run—if there is a long run—he will probably respect you for your loyalty to her and may come around to accepting her when he sees that she's no threat to him.

The same sort of diplomacy is in order when your girl friend teams up with a boy you don't like. About the worst thing you can do is disparage him to her. If their relationship continues, it can only mean the end of yours. Instead, try to like him *because* she likes him. You know the expression, "Any friend of Mary's is a friend of mine"? This is the kind of acceptance you ought to consider. If you can't work out your dislike, see her alone.

You might, on the other hand, like Mary's boyfriend all too well. Need I mention that a friend doesn't flirt with her girl friends' boy friends? I think I do, because so many of you do just that. But what does it prove if the boy friend turns to you? That you are more attractive than your friend? And what do you get for it? You're minus a girl friend and plus a boy friend who's pretty sure to leave you as soon as some other girl decides to steal him.

Breaking up friendships. Having talked about getting and keeping friends, we now come up against the painful problem of ending friendships. In a time of such vast and fast development as occurs in the teen years, you are almost certain to outgrow some of your friendships. Perhaps you've taken on new interests that your friends from kindergarten days cannot share. Maybe a friend whom you once admired now seems, in the light of new ideas and associations, to be less admirable. Possibly, you've been led into a master-slave relationship and you feel the need to get off that leash.

Sandy had been friends for several years with Jane, who had

begun to tear her down, to snip away at her confidence. Jane not only criticized Sandy's clothes and hair, but deprecated all her attempts to improve herself intellectually. One of Jane's typical remarks was, "You don't need to read that book. You'll never understand it anyway." Sandy put up with it because their friendship was a habit. Finally she realized that she was never happy when Jane was around though she felt fine with other girls. Hoping to salvage the friendship, she told Jane how she felt, but Jane continued to put her down. "I'm the only one who tells you the truth," Jane kept insisting. "I'm only looking out for your good."

Sandy reasoned that being a target for Jane's darts couldn't possibly do her any good. She stopped calling Jane and tried to avoid seeing her. But Jane came on even more strongly, her hostility worse than ever, until Sandy wisely told her that she wanted to end their friendship.

When a friendship is no longer enjoyable on any level, and surely when it is destructive, it's time to cut the ties. Often a friendship, like a plant, dies a natural death from lack of nurturing. But sometimes the roots must be pulled out forcibly. Breaking a friendship is always painful and should be only a last resort—after every attempt has been made to keep it healthy and flourishing. New friendships may be stimulating, but old friendships are comfortable and satisfying. There's room for both kinds. As we find new friends, our old friendships can become more and more precious. A change of interests, status or locale is not a signal to drop all your old friends. As you begin to associate with more immediately compatible girls, some of your old friendships will lapse and others will mellow.

There is no law that says your friends must be carbon copies of you. In fact, you would be a pretty narrow person if you didn't have friends from different backgrounds and with different attitudes from yours. You may not become bosom buddies, but you can have mutually rewarding friendships with people of all ages, of both sexes, from all over the world and from both sides of the track. As I said earlier, you don't usually choose a friend *because* she's different. But just as important, you should never shrink from developing a potential friendship with someone who doesn't fit the pattern you're accustomed to. When you stick to friends who think and dress and talk the way you do, you're missing a chance to enrich yourself—something like eating nothing but chicken and rice seven dinners a week. (There are people who do just that, but life isn't very exciting for them.) Similarly, the snob who weeds out all her old friends as she climbs the ladder of social success loses out on the warmth and joy of long-time, old-shoe friendships.

Think carefully before breaking a friendship. Once you have decided it's the right thing to do, do it with all possible honesty and tact. If you can, let it end not with a bang but a whimper. And once you've ended a friendship, for goodness' sake, don't consider it open season on spilling out all the confidences your ex-friend has ever told you. It is always graceless and unladylike to tell tales about a former friend. Your other friends will wonder what you're going to say about them. Besides, it makes you look foolish for having been a friend of that "awful" person.

Try to avoid turning a former friend into a current enemy. Remember the good times you had, and in respect for them be gracious.

There is no phase of friendship that doesn't offer problems. But most of us feel that friends are worth the effort it takes to make and keep them.

Does a Good Date Make a Good Mate?

How would you like me to give you a magic word that will help you to choose the right husband and make a successful marriage?

The word is *dating,* but in order to make it work, you'll have to use it wisely.

From a psychological viewpoint, dating is a healthy custom —arising from our country's concept of individual liberty—that gives you the chance to choose your lifetime partner on the basis of your own needs and desires. The underlying idea is that by getting to know many young men, you will eventually be able to make an educated choice of the one you will marry.

But with freedom comes responsibility. As with all free choices, you have the same opportunity to make the wrong one as the right one. So the dating system can work either for you or against you. If you use dating as an end in itself—as a game or a popularity contest—you're likely to miss out on its most important function.

One young lady I was counseling worked hard to get a certain high school halfback to take her out. When I asked her motives, she replied, "He's really pretty square, but all the other girls think he's absolutely terrific. And when I walk into that dance with him, everybody's eyes will fall out!"

It may look funny in print, but you know how common this attitude is. I'm sure it's no news to you that dating has become a "status symbol." You girls live it, but we professionals have a name for it: our studies show that most high school and college students date according to a pattern we call the "dating-rating system."

One study made at a midwestern university revealed that almost all invitations to date were extended and accepted with a view to raising one's prestige. Thus, if you dated someone with a higher rating than yours, your own rating would go up. And vice versa.

What were these ratings based on?

The Top Date, according to the study, would have been a tall, well-built, even-featured, well-dressed and cheerful young man who was captain of the football team, editor of the school paper and president of his class. Such a paragon might have attained his campus position because of certain qualities that would also make a good husband. But there was little in the rating to indicate that the girls were specifically interested in those qualities.

In another published study, eleventh graders were asked what they looked for in a date. The girls listed in order of importance:

1. personality
2. ability to get along with people
3. good physique
4. good conversation
5. good listener

And the boys listed similar things in slightly different order, placing "nice-looking" in second position and "considerate" in third.

I recently asked forty college sophomore girls for the characteristics they preferred in their dates. The top five choices were surprisingly similar:

1. handsome
2. good personality
3. considerate
4. respectful
5. good manners

Later I asked the same girls the qualities they would most desire in a husband. These lists were, for the most part, quite different. The five most frequent preferences were:

1. considerate
2. same religion
3. respectful
4. money
5. intelligent

Since the girls wrote "money" rather than "rich," I interpret this category as meaning "ability to support a family." From the difference in these five points alone, it appears that more superficial aspects are considered important for dating than for marriage. But what strikes me is the indication that many girls don't seem to understand the relationship between dating and marriage. They don't see dating as a way of meeting and evaluating future husbands. Yet most girls end up marrying boys they chose as dates—for the superficial qualities they listed. Some of those boys turn out to be excellent husbands, but I can't help feeling that some of the girls would actually have been better off letting their parents arrange their marriages. And how about all the good husband material that scores low in the dating-rating game? How many marital prizes go to the girls who don't rate high enough to get the dating champions?

Quite apart from a boy's rating as a date, a girl would be wise to consider his honesty, ambitiousness, sensitivity, loyalty, stability, his willingness to accept responsibility and his love for children. For these are some of the qualities found in men who make good husbands.

Does a good date make a good mate? It's up to you to find out. Since you're lucky enough to live in a time and a place that permits you to choose your husband, do make the choice wisely. I have so often heard the phrase: "But I didn't know what he was really like until we were married." The sad part of this excuse is that there's no excuse for it.

There are a number of ways to discover through dating what a young man is really like (and if *you* really like him). These rules and your own good judgment could be your not-so-magic key to successful marriage.

1. *Be yourself.* Sometimes from fear of rejection, sometimes from thoughtlessly adopting a "crowd personality," a girl puts forth an image of herself that isn't true. We all relate differently to different people, and various dates will bring out different aspects of your personality. (Isn't "falling in love" what happens when you find someone who brings out the best in you?) But there is a big difference between natural reaction and unnatural play-acting.

A girl becomes aware of a boy's likes and dislikes and, often without knowing it, she begins to play up to his preferences. If she thinks he likes "intellectuals," she may pretend to be bookish. Or if she feels it will make her more popular, she might act the coquette though she's really a tomboy. But there's no point in trying to win a boy on false representation. It's foolish to claim you adore football when you really don't. How much more considerate—of your date and yourself—to admit your feelings and say you'll go to some games anyway because you enjoy his company.

If you don't build up false illusions, there won't be any dis-illusionment.

And while you're being yourself, you might also avoid becoming a carbon copy of your boy friend, echoing his opinions, attitudes and interests. Successfully married people do have many interests in common but—just as important—they have individual interests too.

2. *Broaden your date base.* It's a mistake to date just one type of boy. The girl who dates exclusively by dating-rating standards will have very little variety to choose from. Not only is it more fun to know many different kinds of people, but it helps to develop your own personality as well. A reserved boy who doesn't impress your crowd in general may have a lot to offer you in particular. A newcomer from another part of the world may be so interesting that a date with him is well worth a bit of struggle with language. There's little you can learn by sticking always to one group with similar tastes and ideas. We live in a big world.

I'm sure you have guessed by now that I don't think much of "going steady" at an early age. It obviously defeats the very purpose of dating. When I have questioned girls who have "gone steady" (with one or more boys) during high school and even junior high, one fact has almost always emerged: they did it because they felt insecure. But look at the price they pay for the security of a Saturday night date every week. They lose the chance to meet other boys, to learn to get along with different people, to learn more about themselves by exposure to new ideas and situations.

3. *Change the scene.* Say you have dated for a while and have found a boy you really enjoy being with. He likes you the way you are and you like him the way you think he is. Your crowd likes him and even your parents approve. So you go bowling every Friday night and to the movies every Saturday night. You know his taste in movies and his bowling score. But you'd better find out a lot more before you think in permanent terms.

A date is usually a set-up situation where you see each other at your dressed-up, smiling best. Marriage isn't at all like that, and it's good to know in advance how your husband might react if the oven broke down just before his boss was expected for dinner.

You should make it a point to see each other in many different situations. Try new people and new places. Even in a small town, there are plenty of different things to do. The two of you can stage a barbecue or a formal dinner party, take a long bike ride and picnic, get up a play-reading group, go to a city theater, do some volunteer work together. Variety ought to be the spice of dating.

4. *Be alone together.* Like all popular customs, "double-dating" arose from a need. Another couple provides moral support, keeps up conversation, often adds to the fun and—many girls feel —reduces the risk of getting into a petting session. I think that double-dating is a fine ice-breaker and going out in a crowd can be great fun. But after a few such dates, it's a good idea to mix in some "single dates."

I have almost stopped being surprised to learn from an engaged couple that they have never been out alone together. It's hard to imagine a courtship entirely *en masse* and it's hard to imagine a worse way to prepare for marriage. Since most of married life is spent alone together, Mrs. Joe should learn in advance what Joe is like without his buddies to back him up all evening.

Even if you're strictly casual about your dates, it's good practice to be on your own sometimes. You may find it brings out new dimensions in both you and your escort.

5. *Bring on the family.* Many teen-agers rush their dates in and out of the house as if their parents had a contagious disease. I know that some parents tend to put a young man on the witness stand and others to forget to treat their daughter as the near grownup she is. But a good date won't mind.

If you're squeamish about boy-meets-parents occasions, ask yourself why. Could it be you're afraid they'll criticize him or disapprove of your dating him? Are you worried that they'll reveal some of your own faults you've tried to keep under cover? Or is this perhaps a part of your life that you want your parents to keep out of?

I knew a girl who *never* went out with boys of her own religion, though she dated many boys. She insisted it was coincidence, but while her friends found many acceptable boys within this religious group, she never did. After several years, she awakened to the fact that she was using her choice of dates as a club to punish her parents, who felt strongly about staying within one's religious group. When she recognized her motives, she became able to express her resentment more directly and then could date on a more rational basis.

I feel that when you've thought it over honestly—remembering that your parents are grownups and that they wish you well —you'll want to pull down that quarantine sign. Certainly an evening or a day at home is in order for any boy you've dated for a while.

6. *Go slowly.* A relationship that starts with necking can get physically out of control before it even gets going mentally. Most girls today feel that some physical display of affection has a place in dating, but few would want to get trapped in a relationship that's *all* physical. Many studies reported in psychological literature indicate that you have a better chance of marital success if there is no extensive sexual experience before marriage.

So it's smart to be physically reticent. A slow-budding romance produces a firmer blossom than the whirlwind variety and helps to prevent your confusing physical attraction with love.

7. *Don't be a reformer.* Some women are forever trying to change themselves—constantly revising hairdos, wardrobes, hobbies, home decorations—all in search of an identity that doesn't exist. I'm not talking about thoughtful efforts to improve themselves; I mean the kind of basic dissatisfaction that is expressed in perpetual discontent with things as they are.

I hope none of you girls will turn into that kind of woman because she can never be truly happy. We must accept ourselves as we are and then work from there to improve where improvement is possible. The same principle applies to the boys you go out with: you cannot make them over to fit an ideal that exists only in your mind. Either accept your date as he is, or mark him off as one who won't make a good mate for you.

If your date seems to be lazy or self-centered, if he has a violent temper or a drinking problem, you'd be deluding yourself to think his love for you is going to change him.

On the other hand, if a date you like doesn't quite conform to your ideal, you might consider changing your ideal to fit him: it's easier and healthier.

8. *Take a backward look.* If you think a boy may have a place in your future, learn something about his past. It doesn't require detective work: most people, as they get to know other people, start talking about themselves and their families. If a frequent date seems to gloss over his life before he met you, you have a right to wonder why.

No date would mind your taking a polite interest in his background—unless he were keeping something from you, something that might give you reason to stop seeing him. Tact is indeed a virtue, but it can be carried too far. Married men *have* led girls to believe they were eligible bachelors. Delinquents *have* passed themselves off as model gentlemen. You have not only a right but a duty to yourself to know whom you're dating and where he comes from.

Almost all studies show that people of similar religious and social backgrounds have a head start toward marital happiness. Also, young people brought up by happily married parents have a better chance than those who grew up in broken homes. While choosing someone with a different background from yours doesn't necessarily foredoom your marriage, it does increase the obstacles for you to cross. You may decide that it's worth the risk. But you should make the decision with your eyes open.

9. *Take your time.* Whoever coined the phrase, "Marry in haste, repent at leisure," knew what he was talking about. As a child, did you ever yearn for a toy that, once possessed, made you wonder why you had been so eager for it? It would be much, much worse if you were to feel that way about engagement or marriage.

You will do a lot of growing up in the years after high school, and it's not unusual for the boy who seemed tops when you were both sophomores to be a good deal less appealing when you have reached voting age. Tastes change—and *should* change—rather rapidly at your age. If you taste in dates changes, you'll do better not to be tied down. And if it doesn't change, then it's probably love and you'll both still be there.

There is a close relationship between length of courtship and a successful marriage. In 1890 the average marrying age for men was twenty-six and for women twenty-two. In 1960 it was twenty-three for men and a little under twenty for girls. During that time, the divorce rate has steadily risen. It's something to think about, isn't it?

Each phase—dating, going steady, engagement—offers its special satisfactions, serves its special purpose. Why not enjoy each to the fullest, without rushing into the next?

10. *Face facts.* Before every marriage that explodes or withers into divorce, there were warning signs that for one reason or another were ignored or pushed aside. In spite of ourselves—or perhaps *to* spite ourselves—we all walk into trouble sometimes. And sometimes we play the ostrich by hiding our head in the sand. Sooner or later we have to look up, and we find ourselves facing the same problems that sent us hiding in the first place. Problems don't disappear, but ostriches are on their way to extinction.

The failure to face a fault in a boy friend or a flaw in a relationship comes understandably from fear. If you refuse this date, when will you get another? If you return this pin, what will you tell your friends? If you break your engagement, how can you explain to your family? And how could you hurt *him* so deeply?

But a bird in the hand isn't worth anything if it's going to bite you. A few raised eyebrows or I-told-you-so's will cause you much less pain than will an unhappy marriage. And a clean break sooner is much kinder to *him* than the drawn-out suffering that seems in store for later.

So face facts and share your fears. Perhaps when your problems are brought into the open, they won't be so great as you think. Certainly your date deserves to know what's on your mind and in your heart. For he, too, is trying to answer the question: Does a good date make a good mate?

Why Your Parents Don't Understand You

Among a group of well-adjusted, achieving college sophomores, more than half the girls recently admitted a definite feeling that their parents do not understand them. For younger teen-agers, the percentage would probably be a good deal higher. As primary causes of friction, the college girls listed:

1. My parents don't understand that I'm grown up.
2. They don't understand my choice of friends or dates.
3. They don't appreciate my need to be alone at times.
4. They don't recognize my ability to make decisions.
5. They don't understand my idealism.

I'm sure you can imagine—and probably recall—family squabbles that arise from these causes: your father refusing to let you take the car; your mother fretting over the hours you spend on the phone with friends she considers either "too silly" or "too bold"; your father wanting you to join a family outing when you'd rather be with friends; your mother begging "please look at the *practical* side of it"; both harping at you to be something you aren't and don't want to become.

Many of your complaints are valid and boil down to a gap between your parents' image of you and your own idea of yourself. Far from being spiteful or unconcerned, however, most parents want to understand you but are prevented by factors in their own lives and backgrounds.

Their dreams and hopes for you. You've probably heard the "Soliloquy" from *Carousel,* in which a baritone sings about the rugged man's man his son is going to be when he grows up:

> My boy Bill will be tall and as tough as a tree . . .
> But he'll have more common sense than his puddin'-
>   headed father ever had . . .*

The child in question "ain't even been born yet."

This is typical of a parent's reaction to the news of a coming baby. He immediately begins to spin a web of dreams and hopes. You've seen toddlers wearing polo shirts that read *Harvard 1987*, preschool girls wearing nylon stockings. And, of course, there's the scene from the Grade B movie where the new father approaches the hospital nursery carrying football and tennis racket. There's scarcely a parent—especially in this society of success stories—who doesn't cherish some fond dreams about the important person his child will be. Most parents, as their children grow up, modify their dreams to fit the reality of the children's personalities and abilities. Some parents are more reluctant than others to give up dreams of their children's success, particularly if their own lives have been marked with disappointment. If your father couldn't go to college because he had to go to work to support his family, he may yearn for you to get your degree. If your mother felt shy and out of things as a teen-ager, she may be zealously eager for you to be one of the "best" crowd.

The trouble starts when you are unable or unwilling to fulfill your parents' wishes. They may feel disappointed in you or they may feel they have failed as parents.

The difference in age. Your parents may be from eighteen to forty years older than you are and that much different from you physically and mentally. This gives rise to many problems.

You might play a game of tennis in the morning, swim all afternoon and be ready to dance all evening. Your father, on the other hand, might make it through tennis and an afternoon dip, but by nighttime he will probably have had it. No wonder he's aghast when you say, "I won't be back till very late tonight." Quite possibly he'll complain that you're running yourself ragged. That's how *he'd* feel if he were in your party shoes.

Furthermore, in those twenty or forty years they have on you, your parents have learned something about people and places and things. They know from experience many of the things you're just trying on for size. *They* would like to use their experience to protect you from being hurt; *you* feel they're only throwing water on the flames of your enthusiasm.

You come back from a summer job interview, thrilled. "He said he's got to see some other people first, but he likes me and he'll call in a few days."

Your father says, somewhat grimly: "Keep looking, honey. He may never call."

You're hurt by this gloomy pessimism, while he—who has been through the don't-call-me-I'll-call-you routine—thinks he's helping you to avoid disappointment.

Your mother, too, has been storing up trials and errors since her own teens and wants very much to give you the benefit of her experience. Perhaps the boy you're currently flipping over reminds her of someone she used to date. He turned out to be a false alarm and your mother is full of warnings about your boy friend. *You* think her protective instincts are going to keep you from getting any firsthand experience of your own. *She* thinks she would be failing you as a mother if she didn't use her seasoned judgment to help you out.

In fact, of course, her experiences date from another time. Some of what she learned is still valid; some is not.

You're in high gear. As your parents grow a year older, they seem to you not to have changed a bit. But during the same year, you may have changed into someone they hardly recognize. What is important to you this year may not have taken a second thought twelve months ago. It is usually difficult for parents to keep up with the current you.

Just as you sometimes find your life as a teen-ager challenging and confusing, so do they find their roles as parents to a teen-ager. It takes time to adjust to the "new you."

Difference in backgrounds. You change and times change too. Your parents very likely grew up during the depression of the thirties and were teen-agers during World War II, years when money was short, goods were scarce, travel was limited and most people were less sophisticated than most people are now. They grew up before television, before the formation of the United Nations and before the age of nuclear physics—in a much simpler world than yours is today. Going by the last generation's standards of frugality and comparative provincialism, your parents may see your crowd as extravagant, fast and oversophisticated.

They may also tend to oversimplify your problems. Going by recipe books on how-to-get-along-with-your-teen-agers, they may try to reduce your experience to a "phase" or a "quirk" or a "whim." Hoping for easy answers, they may simply refuse to take you seriously.

It's important to remember that some ideas—like dress lengths and hair styles—come and go with fashion. Most parents try to keep up with the times, but it isn't easy to avoid hangovers of old ways of thinking. Such hangovers can be hard to get around. If your mother was taught to believe that women belong in the home, you can hardly blame her for questioning your plans to study marine biology at a college halfway across the country. That doesn't mean, however, that you shouldn't go.

Problems in their own lives. As a child, you tended to idealize your parents—to see them as closer to perfect than they really were. As you proceed through your teens, the pendulum swings in the opposite direction until you see your parents as just about impossible. When you are older, a balanced, more realistic picture of your parents as people comes into view.

Like all other people, your parents have their own particular sets of problems and defenses and anxieties and insecurities. Sometimes (very much like you) they can cope with their problems pretty well. But at times of stress, those problems are likely to spill over into their relationship with you.

Your family has moved from the security of an old, familiar neighborhood into a strange, new part of the country; there is a serious illness in the family; your father is away on an extended business trip; your younger brother is failing fourth grade: can you see that any of these situations might make your mother more irritable than usual?

Your father has recently changed jobs; his doctor has told him to cut down on his activities; the candidate whose election he has been working for goes down in defeat: you know that he is less likely to be sympathetic to your projects at times like these than during a period of smooth sailing.

Early experiences leave most people with some wounds, over which scar tissue has grown, and which cause trouble when difficulties arise. Very often, these early experiences set up patterns that endure long after the need for them has ended, causing people to behave in what seems to be an unreasonable way. Latent fears become aroused and your parents may suddenly seem *hyper*critical, *over*protective, *un*reasonably demanding.

The girl whose mother agrees to buy her a new dress for the prom and then produces one excuse after another to avoid doing it can't understand such stinginess. Her father says he can easily spare the money. Finally, her mother insists the daughter wear a dress she bought three months ago. The mother says she can't understand her daughter's extravagance.

A reason for the mother's attitude is suggested by a look at her background. Raised in a very frugal household, she naturally built upon a pattern of never wasting anything. Thrift became a necessary way of life. Now, though there is plenty of money, her old instincts for frugality make it impossible for her to be free and easy in spending.

Broken connections. Some families are more accustomed than others to talking things over. But too often—even in the most open of families—the teen-ager chooses to assert her independence by clamming up. Sometimes, too, parents hide their problems and true feelings under a great deal of chatter; no real messages get through the static.

Slammed doors or abruptly halted conversations with friends can make your mother wonder what's the big secret. How many times has a parent come into a room and heard you say into the telephone: "I can't talk now. I'll call you later." This kind of broad hint can—depending upon your parents' personalities—make them doubly curious or hurt and silent.

You may feel shy about discussing certain topics with your parents or you may be afraid that they'll use your confidences against you, possibly take over completely on a problem when you only want a little sympathy or advice. So you say nothing. After a few months of skirting the issue, the habit of secrecy is on you and you find that the process of communication has broken down almost completely.

One girl recently told me that her parents didn't understand her because they never asked her about anything that was really important to her. What she negelected to mention was her habitually hostile reaction to questions. Her parents had received the message—all too well.

How you can help. Hundreds of articles and books, many of them excellent, have been written to help parents understand teen-agers, but in my experience, nothing can be quite so effective as your trying to help *your* parents to understand you. Regardless of why your parents seem to be unsympathetic, here are nine tips that may help you help them see things your way.

1. *Understand them.* Being human, your parents have idiosyncrasies, pet peeves or blind spots; and if you venture into that territory, you *know* they're going to see red. I'm not suggesting that you knuckle under on major issues, but I think a lot of family strife can be averted if you can simply learn to avoid waving a red flag before the bull.

Example: If your mother has a "thing" about neatness (and some mothers can overdo this routine), it wouldn't compromise you to straighten up your room before school in the morning. If your father hates the Monkees, it's only sensible (not to say considerate) of you to turn down the phonograph when he's around. There is no point in making big issues over small disagreements. Pinpoint your parents' weak spots and tread lightly thereon.

Try also to understand your parents' *patterns* of behavior. Your mother is likely to be particularly edgy the day that she's giving a dinner party. Your father may come home irritable from fighting five o'clock traffic. Don't ask your mother to hem your dress on her party day; wait till after dinner before mentioning a not-too-brilliant report card to Dad.

2. *Understand yourself.* Few people genuinely understand themselves, what they really want and even how they really feel.

Jill D. thinks her mother is picking on her because Mrs. D. constantly complains that Jill wears too much make-up. One day, a good friend suggests that Jill would look a lot better without the heavy shadow and eyeliner for daytime wear. Jill arrives at school less overpainted, her new look is generally complimented and she realizes that her mother *wasn't* just looking for a fight. She also realizes she would have made the change long ago if she hadn't been so stubborn about taking her mother's advice.

It's not easy to admit unpleasant things about ourselves. Are you sometimes moody and uncooperative? Do you put your needs before the needs of anyone else in the family? Do you expect your parents' lives to rotate around your own activities? When you start asking yourself questions like this, you have taken a step on the road to self-understanding.

3. *Communicate with them.* Yes, you deserve your privacy and nobody (not even your parents) has the right to know *everything* about you. But many girls are unnecessarily secretive.

Your privacy is not really being violated if you tell your mother something about last night's school dance. It's fun for her to know how the gym was decorated and she would enjoy knowing which boys asked you to dance.

Actually, a willingness to talk things over with parents is a sign of maturity. Your own reports often bring on tales of their experiences, and in the ensuing exchange you may gain the position not of a little girl but of a friend.

Asking for advice in certain areas might help your mother to leave you to your own decisions in others. Perhaps if she knew that you came to her when you wanted her advice, she'd save it for the times when you asked. There's no reason to fear that one consultation with a parent will lead to a takeover. You might even find your parent summing up both sides of a problem and turning the decision over to you. Sometimes an objective, adult view is just what you need to clarify your thinking.

If your problem is that your parents treat you as a baby, the sensible way to work it out is to tell your parents how you feel. A calm discussion at an appropriate time and place will give you a chance to explain your resentment of being "bossed" and "clucked over." Your parents may be very much surprised to learn how you feel and you may learn something about their reasons for concern over you. Just as high-level diplomacy is necessary to build understanding between nations, so should policy talks help to keep the peace within your family.

4. *A little loving goes a long way.* Everybody needs to be loved, and that includes parents.

Under the pressure of their need to find a place in the world, teen-agers often forget to show love. In fact, it's not unusual for them to treat parents as if they were pieces of furniture, hired hands or even unsightly blotches on the horizon.

There are reasons for this kind of behavior. Teen-agers are usually more important to their parents than their parents are to them. Ours is a child-centered society and many parents—mothers particularly—have failed to find satisfying outside interests. A teen-ager may be so eager not to lean on her parents that she figuratively pushes them away from her. Some parents are wise enough to understand this mechanism and to lie low for a while, but many others feel hurt and rejected. It's wise to remember that if you put your parents down, they may not bounce right back.

Family life can't be—and probably shouldn't be—a prolonged meeting of the Mutual Admiration Society. But there are doubtless many opportunities for showing kindness and affection that you've been overlooking lately.

5. *Each to his own taste.* A frequent complaint goes like this: "My parents won't let me have my own likes and dislikes." The complaint is usually valid; most parents do tend to try to inflict their tastes upon their children.

Then the teen-ager goes on to say, ". . . and my parents' taste is not to be believed! My father watches Westerns on television. My mother plays canasta twice a week, if you can imagine it. And they have parties with these silly friends who don't even know what's going on in the world . . ."

You see, don't you, that this girl is doing to her parents *exactly what she resents their doing to her?* She wants them to respect her activities and opinions, but she refuses to accept theirs.

It is not true that "there is no accounting for tastes"; likes and dislikes are based on our total life experience. Your parents' experiences, having been different from yours, may well generate likes and dislikes that make little sense to you. A woman may compensate for her childhood feelings of deprivation by collecting expensive antiques that you think are hideous. A man who gives what you consider too much attention to sports may need this outlet to offset frustrations at his business office.

Furthermore, parents use relaxation in a way that few teenagers are equipped to understand. Dad may not patronize TV Western as an art form but as a good way to sit back for an hour and watch the Good Guy win for a change. No, the Western doesn't challenge him any more than canasta challenges Mom. Both are relaxing to *escape* challenge. Most teen-agers don't appreciate this kind of recreation. You are "on" all the time. You don't want to *watch* a story. You want to *live* it. You want to *be* the man on the white horse and you think you can. Parents have been fighting the battle for a long time and sometimes their taste in leisure is just about the opposite from that of a teen-ager who is still choosing up sides.

The disdain or angry disapproval of a daughter can take a lot of the kick out of parents' fun. I remember an impromptu jitterbug session that took place at the home of friends after a small dinner party. Their fifteen-year-old daughter was embarrassed at her parents' cavorting, and the seventeen-year-old was distressed. "If you weren't so square," she commented, "you'd be silly."

Yet the lindy and the shag are no sillier than the frug, the monkey or the watusi. It's a matter of times and taste. The daughter who wants to assert her own individuality might start by accepting her parents as individuals.

6. *Show how mature you are.* Everybody wants freedom, but too few of us want the responsibility that comes with it.

Your parents' job is to take care of you until you are able to take care of yourself. You want to take care of yourself before they think you are ready to do so. Or you want to take care of yourself in certain areas and you want them to take over the rest of the time. Or you want to take care of yourself in a way that your parents don't think is very careful. Or any of a dozen variations of the conflict over dependency and independence, rules and laissez-faire, supervision and freedom.

On the whole, parents loosen the reins as they feel their daughters are able to handle new responsibilities. If you want more freedom, then, the best way to get it is to show that you can take responsibility. For example: Jane, a high school sophomore, wanted to go out with Bill, a junior, in his car. Jane's mother had not met Bill before this first date and was concerned about his driving ability and his character. Jane assured her mother that Bill was a careful driver and a boy of fine reputation, and eventually her mother gave in—*provided* Jane was home by midnight.

Jane and Bill went off to an amusement park. At eleven-thirty, Jane suggested starting for home, but Bill, with four tickets left, persuaded her to take a ride on the whip and another on the caterpillar. Then he suggested a soda and Jane, having a wonderful time, went right along. You know the rest. When Jane walked in at one-thirty, her parents were frantic with worry and about to phone the police.

You can't blame Jane's mother for calling a halt to car dates after that. If Jane had made a prompt midnight appearance, or had telephoned, her mother would have been likely to let the bars of protection down another notch or two.

Mothers are very proud to say, "I let Susan have a great deal of freedom because she's very conscientious. If she's late coming home from school, she always calls to let me know where she is. Her friends' mothers have told me that she conducts herself very well at parties, and she uses good judgment at home. I trust her completely."

It's easier for parents to say yes to your results than to have to wrangle. But broken promises, lapses of memory, half-finished jobs and other displays of irresponsibility may convince them that a no is necessary. If you want to be treated as an adult, try to behave like one.

Your mother won't buy you a new dress for the prom? You've explained your point of view and she still doesn't see it? How about earning the money and buying it yourself? Your father won't let you go to your steady beau's college weekend? You've told him that fifty other girls' fathers have said yes? You've assured him that the party will be chaperoned and that the girls will stay at a sorority house and be subject to house rules?

You've offered to pay for transportation out of your savings? Perhaps the boy's mother would talk to your mother.

If nothing works, you'll have to give in. While you are living in your parents' home, they must be the final authority on important questions. Graceful surrender rather than sulking may show your parents you're more mature than they'd thought.

7. *Show them where your roads converge.* You and your parents may often disagree on the means to an end while being in accord about the end itself. Before you start battling, let them know that you are basically in agreement.

Your parents want you to go to a certain small, all-girl college. You want to go to a huge, coed university. Start off with the announcement "I'm not going to Small College" and you immediately get their backs up. But begin the conversation gently, with "I know you want me to get a good education, but I think I would do better at Big U." Have your reasons ready—perhaps a Big U catalogue to show them what you mean—and you may not only avert a quarrel but possibly also get your way.

In any disagreement, you and your parents are more likely to understand one another if you accentuate the positive before you try to eliminate the negative.

8. *Pitch in on their projects.* You may not see how anyone could possibly get enjoyment from spending a hot afternoon on his knees in the garden setting out dahlia tubers. But this may be exactly what your father likes to do. If you want to assure him of your love and respect, there's probably no better way than to put in a half-hour out there beside him. Spontaneous behavior

is great, but sometimes calculation is in order. In families—as in life—certain techniques are helpful in smoothing out rough spots.

If your mother is having the bridge club for supper, she'd appreciate your offer to mix up a salad or set the table. Family living is a cooperative setup and your cheerful, voluntary cooperation helps to keep everyone in good humor. Your own activities and projects probably keep you pretty well occupied, but you really enter into the family spirit when you put some of your parents' interests before your own "I want" and "I like."

9. *Remember parents are people, too.* Try the Golden Rule in reverse: "Do not do to your parents what you would not want them to do to you." If you do not want them to speak crossly to you, try speaking gently to them. If you don't want them to order you about, stop ordering them about. If you don't want to be criticized, don't criticize them. If you want dispensations, remember your obligations.

If nothing works, if your home life is an agony that you can do nothing to abate, you may be quite right in feeling that your parents—or one of them—are incapable of reasonable behavior. When you see unhealth around you, you can make up your mind to do better when you are a parent. Meanwhile, whatever your feelings, your actions must still take into account the fact that you are living under their authority. You would do well to think of going to an out-of-town college or to get a job away from home as soon as you are graduated from high school and legally old enough to live away.

Remember that your feelings and tastes cannot be dictated.

If you are marching to the sound of "a different drummer," keep your ears open. Notwithstanding the respect that is due to your parents, you may decide to go against their wishes. But remember that you will be proceeding at your own risk.

If your parents understand you, you're a lucky girl. And if they don't, try to give them all the help you can. Often it will be enough to get you through your teens with a minimum of family turmoil.

The One and Only You

In legendary Greece, there lived a cruel robber named Procrustes. He kept a wayside inn, where the unwary traveler was put up for the night in a special iron bed. Naturally, one bed did not exactly fit all the travelers; so Procrustes made *them* fit the bed. If they were too tall, he cut off their feet; if they were too short, he stretched them. What Procrustes insisted upon was conformity.

Sometimes a teen-ager feels that everyone—her parents, her school and her community—is trying to squeeze her into a Procrustean bed. Sometimes she is her own Procrustes, so caught up in thinking and doing what she thinks is expected of her that she fails to consider her own wants and needs. Individualism versus conformity is not just a teen-age problem, but it is a problem particularly troublesome to teen-agers. When to—and when not to—go along with the crowd, protest an order that seems unjust, follow tradition or buck the system are important decisions. Finding your own healthy balance between conformity and individualism is crucial to the kind of growing up you do and the kind of adult you will be.

In a number of situations, conformity is useful and necessary.

Obeying rules is our payment for the convenience of living among other people in relative safety and comfort. Traffic regulations are necessary for efficient travel, rules of grammar permit effective communication, laws of property allow us to live in harmony with our neighbors.

Following custom often simplifies daily living. Etiquette, for example, facilitates social life. If you decided to be completely individualistic about your table manners, you would be faced with a half-dozen decisions every time you sat down to dinner. When you've spent a weekend with relatives, you know that a bread-and-butter note will fulfill your obligation to everyone's satisfaction. The customary amenities make for smooth social situations.

Observing convention makes us feel secure. Conventional morality, which grows out of general sociological needs, is aimed at achieving the greatest good for the greatest number of people. Conventional behavior is the way things are done by most of the people most of the time. Obviously, conventions change as "the old order changeth, yielding place to new." But following familiar patterns not only frees us from constant decision-making, it also provides us with a feeling of well-being.

Conformity, therefore, is useful in its place. What is diminishing to a personality and dangerous to a society is *thoughtless* conformity: squeezing into a slot that is not your size; blindly obeying foolish rules; mechanically following customs when the situation calls for a sincere expression of feeling; accepting conventions that are no longer relevant; sticking to habits that are no longer satisfying.

Do you know an overconformist? She's the girl whose mind is made up as soon as she knows what others are thinking. Her principle reason for doing things is that "That's the way things are done."

Eventually, she loses contact with her own thoughts and feelings. It becomes almost impossible for her to act spontaneously. Unless there are people to tell her what to think or feel, she feels empty, indecisive and dissatisfied with life.

The underconformist *seems* to be her opposite. To her, the majority is always wrong. If bell-bottoms are the word, she'll parade herself in a party dress. If all the girls are Sean Connery fans, she can't bear him. She is the standout in any group, the holdout in any project. Yet, in latching on to unpopular people and unpopular causes (regardless of their merit), the under-conformist is no more spontaneous or rational than the over-conformist. She, too, is overly influenced by her surroundings; but her reaction is reversed.

The girl who conforms rationally knows who she is and what she really wants. She can enjoy trying out new fads and fashions but can also stop short at those she knows are unbecoming to her. She can go along with group attitudes in matters where her sense of integrity is not challenged, but she is also free to express her dissent by either arguing or going her own way. She chooses her friends, her clothes, her clubs, her hobbies, her opinions *on their merits* rather than blindly following or rebelling against other people's choices.

The self-image of a girl in her teens is likely to be tentative, experimental, transient. In trying on attitudes, interests and even personalities for size, she can hardly avoid following others. She tends to be attracted—or repelled—by many outside influences, some of them so different from one another that she may occasionally feel like a chameleon—taking on the color of whatever environment she happens to be in at the moment.

Parents versus "the crowd." During the teen years, the weight of parental authority diminishes and the influence of friends and schoolmates usually increases. When this shift in loyalty occurs, some girls react by rejecting wholesale the attitudes and values of their parents. If Mother says it's good, it's got to be bad. If the crowd says it's right, right it is. Wholesale rebellion against parents may seem to be the height of individuality, but it's often the opposite. The mature individual sees her parents—and her friends—as neither heroes nor villains, but real people. How much they influence her is based on her choice, not compulsive conformity or compulsive rebellion.

The group. You'd probably be surprised at an objective assessment of how much your behavior is affected by a desire to fit in with your group of friends. If your group is one that maintains a sound balance between independence and conformity, you're lucky. Some teen groups, however, specialize in rebellion against anything that has the approval of the adult world. Caught up in such a crowd, you're likely to become a conforming nonconformist and to miss out on the questioning and thinking through that are an important part of discovering yourself.

A path beaten down by others is easier to walk than one through which you have to cut your own way: imitation is easier than innovation.

Your group is likely to have a style of dress that you keep up with, certain speech mannerisms or pet expressions that you adopt, musical tastes and dating patterns that you share. If your crowd smokes, you probably smoke too.

Smoking is a good example of the harm that going along can do. Nobody can honestly say that cigarettes are good for you; nobody is addicted to smoking before going through the first few packs; and I don't know anyone who actually enjoyed her first smoke. There seems to be no good reason for anyone to become a habitual smoker. One of the primary reasons is the wish to be like the rest of the girls in a smoking crowd.

The conformity that causes a girl to adopt group attitudes toward other people is also damaging. Say that two girls in your crowd turn some of their surplus anger on an outsider, Maggie. Without having done anything to justify their wrath, Maggie can very soon become the hate target of the whole crowd. Suddenly you find yourself mocking or slighting Maggie, making her very unhappy for no reason other than to be in on a group activity. The blind conformist simply doesn't stop to think about justice or another girl's feelings.

This process can also be reversed. If everyone in your crowd adores Peter, you may join the competition for his attention without even thinking whether or not *you* like him. And if you win the "prize," you're likely to find yourself dating a boy who is not particularly bright or interesting to you. Dating a boy because your friends think he's dreamy is a fine way to stunt your personality growth, but conformists do it all the time.

How much—and how subtly—many of us are influenced by

the opinions of others is illustrated by a classic experiment conducted among college students. One at a time, the students
were brought into a room and asked to judge the length of a
line. Their first judgments were fairly accurate. But then other
people in the room—all actually working with the testing psychologist—began to talk informally about the length of the line
and to agree upon intentionally outlandish estimates. Upon hearing the other judgments, the subject very often changed his
estimate, moving much closer to the group estimate. In most
cases the subject was *completely unaware* that he had been
influenced by the group.

I'm sure you can apply these findings to yourself. Have you
ever liked a girl less after having heard other girls criticize her?
Have you ever liked a movie more after your friends had pro-
nounced it stupendous? Have you liked a book more after your
teacher or a majority of the class had agreed upon its merits? On
what basis do you decide whether a boy is handsome or homely?
Whether a girl is well-dressed or garish? Aren't your tastes,
opinions, habits of thinking inevitably molded to some degree
by group attitudes? (And similarly, isn't prejudice necessarily an
offshoot of conformity? Without having been influenced from
outside, how else would anyone know enough *in advance* to
dislike a certain racial or national or social group?)

Your society. Most social observers feel that needless conformity is at high tide in the United States. Many factors in our
society foster excessive conformity. Easy money and the oppor-

tunity to improve living standards make social climbers of many people, and whenever anyone is trying to rise to "higher levels" of society, he tends to suffer a great deal of anxiety about his acceptability in the circles to which he aspires. The urge to "get ahead" in business, in a community, in a crowd often makes people submerge the behavior and opinions that they think might hold them back. It's not unusual for families to join a church or a political party, not because the institution relates to their basic feelings, but because "all the right people" are in it. The "upward striving" society produces conformists.

Furthermore, as a nation we are proud of being a "melting pot." Our immigrant population has taken pride in becoming one hundred percent American as soon as possible. While more insular nations may cherish eccentrics, many Americans feel that it is somehow unpatriotic to be "different."

Finally, many people find that the rewards most valued by our society—fame and fortune—are easier to come by if one works to please others rather than oneself. The man who sells a product wanted by most people is much more likely to be financially successful than one who crafts a product to suit himself and perhaps a few others. Mass production not only conforms to mass taste but in turn also *shapes* mass taste, still further extending the area of sameness.

For these among other complex reasons, there's a lot of conformity around. You, however, have a good deal of choice in the degree to which you go along with the trend.

You yourself. It is a human need to be loved and approved of, but one of the most important lessons that we learn as we grow up is that we cannot please all of the people all of the time. The girl who tries to do so rapidly loses all her individual coloration as she blends into one background after another. Popular girls, according to numerous surveys, are distinguished by leadership ability, mastery of skills, liveliness and *originality*. The girl who thinks that conformity will bring everyone's approval is fishing in the wrong pond.

Sometimes overstrict or hypercritical parents or older siblings can reduce a girl's confidence to a sliver. Nobody who has been shouted down or ridiculed whenever she dared speak out is likely to grow up feeling free to express herself. If early experience has left you with a good stock of self-respect, you are less apt to hunger for approval from all directions and better able to act freely.

A sense of security, then, often brings a willingness to make individual decisions. But if you are in a temporarily tenuous position, you may find yourself less courageous than you usually are. If you've recently moved to a new town or a new school or are going through a siege of skin trouble or having a bad time with second-year French, you may find yourself more passive than at times when you feel closer to top form. When you have regained your balance, it will be easier to be yourself. In the same way, the most tentative teen-ager may grow into a confident adult and, with maturity, become relatively free to assert her individuality. Overconformity need not be a chronic condition; it is, however, a good one to outgrow.

Why worry about conformity? It threatens the growth and development of both individuals and society. One major cause of human unhappiness is the wasting of talents or abilities. Undeveloped talents and abilities are a loss to society. Had the Wright brothers been ashamed of being "different," there might not have been a flight at Kitty Hawk. If Frank Lloyd Wright had not dared to diverge from standard architecture, we would not have his buildings and those of his followers to please and stimulate us. All three Wrights had to dare to be wrong.

There is no other person exactly like you. If you try to smooth down all your unique edges in order to match your conception of "the others," you do yourself an injustice. If you disparage the uniqueness of others, you do them and your society a disservice. You will often face challenges to your freedom of expression. In some cases, you may find it convenient or advisable to adapt to your environment. In others, you may have to assert your individuality in order to maintain it. The following pointers may help you to find the balance best suited to the one and only you.

1. *Accept your differences.* Each of you has a personalized list of strong points, weaknesses and in-betweens. How you use your characteristics—physical, mental, emotional—is more important than the characteristics themselves.

Helen and Harriet both have an altitude problem: each is

five feet eleven inches tall in stocking feet. Helen is awkward and retiring; her slumping posture vividly reveals her negative feelings about herself. Harriet, having accepted her height, uses it to her advantage. She dresses beautifully in clothes that emphasize her model's figure. Basically no prettier than Helen, she has made herself into a striking young woman and hopes one day to become a fashion model.

When I was in high school, the best dancer among the boys—and the one most in demand to partner female jitterbugs—was a young man with a limp. Most of us in that school never thought of Harold as anything but a good companion, a fair student and an excellent dancer. It wasn't until two years after graduation when I met Harold on a local street that I saw how seriously he was handicapped. His own lack of self-consciousness and self-pity had made us overlook it.

In the same class was an unusually brilliant girl. Only her closest friends had an inkling of her astronomical IQ. To the rest, she was an average student, occasionally chided by teachers for not doing her best. Sandra felt that "dumb" girls had better dating chances. Continuing to "conform," she took an easy college course instead of one that would challenge her superior intellect, and she was married immediately after graduation. Today Sandra is a discontented housewife who wishes she had "done something" with her life.

2. *Accept differences in others.* Surrounding yourself with people who look alike, dress alike, think alike is akin to spending your life in a hall of mirrors. It is not going to help you broaden

your viewpoint or understanding. It is not going to prepare you for large-scale living. The more you stick to your own kind, the greater will be your discomfort on encountering new people and new ways of looking at things.

Sometimes it's even harder to accept differences in your friends than in yourself. Many girls look for an alter ego, another self, of similar background and tastes, who will agree with every opinion, go along on every project. As soon as a friend shows herself to be anything more than a carbon copy, these girls tend to become disillusioned and to break up the friendship. Other girls no sooner make a new friend than they are after her to lose weight, change her hair style, join the same club, read the same books, like the same people.

A mature friendship, however, includes acceptance of differences as well as enjoyment of similarities. Only when you are tolerant of your friend's individuality can there be an honest relationship between the one and only you and the one and only her.

3. *Know when you're wearing a mask.* Few of us can—or want to—say or act out exactly what we feel in all situations. When a completely frank expression would be unkind, impolite or otherwise inappropriate, people put on a social mask and carry off the scene as gracefully as possible. The important thing is not to confuse the mask with your real face and not to use it unless it is really necessary. If you wear a mask too often, you may start to believe that the character you're playing is really you.

At times you will conform to a distasteful group decision out of courtesy or defeat by majority vote. Sometimes you will be pleasant to disagreeable people and will follow orders you don't believe in. You may take part in customs and ceremonies that have no meaning for you. Learning to comply when necessary—and at the same time to recognize your feelings—is one way to remain true to yourself.

4. *Strike out the unnecessary "shoulds" and "ought to's."* It would be hard to pinpoint a time when teen-agers were more beleaguerd than they are today by demands for top performance, social acceptability, vindication of their parents' lives and personification of their parents' material success. Furthermore, teens are asked to make choices that in other days would have been made for them. I don't say that all of these pressures are necessarily bad, but they are additions to other obligations you feel. Too many "shoulds" make Jane a compulsive girl, often to the detriment of her spontaneity and joy of living.

The healthy thing to do, if you feel overwhelmed by pressures, is to review all activities very carefully. How many of the things you do are you really doing to please or impress someone other than yourself? How many are just habits that can be eliminated without hurting anybody? How many are unfair to you and might be eliminated after a talk with your parents about your feelings on the matter? Why feel obliged to continue with piano lessons if you have no interest in them and little musical talent? Why work toward admission to teachers' college (your parents' choice) when you would prefer to study fashion design? Do you really enjoy dating a certain premed student or do you see him just because your parents like the idea? Do you get pleasure from bowling or do you go along only because the crowd wants you to?

"Want" and "should" are often at odds and it's important to know the difference. Read a book on diplomatic policy because you want to, not only because you feel you should be up on current events. Don't sit through a concert that bores you simply because it seems to be the right thing to do. On the other hand, why cover up a taste for opera because your friends might think it square? Your parents' dream daughter may be very different from the real you; help them to understand and perhaps to share *your* dream for yourself. Everybody needs gratification. When life becomes so full of "shoulds" that "wants" go unsatisfied, the world seems dull and pointless. When you learn to say no to unnecessary demands—and yes to your own needs—you are taking a long step toward healthy maturity.

5. *Develop self-reliance.* Another sign of maturity is the ability to enjoy your own company. If you wait for the crowd to agree on an afternoon of ice skating, you may not get to the rink. If you announce that you're going and then set off, you may get some company. And if nobody joins you, what's wrong with going alone? Why pass up a good movie just because your friends don't care to see it? Why not feel free to shop or walk or go to an event that interests you without being surrounded by a

group? When you travel with friends, you don't see much beyond them. When you move alone, you are better able to stop, look and listen.

A self-reliant girl is strong enough to stand up for a friend or an idea that her crowd disapproves of. She feels free to date a boy they may think "strange" or to pursue a hobby they may consider far out. Often the crowd will come around to accepting her friends and her interests and, at the same time, will respect her independence.

6. *Permit yourself an enemy or two.* More than two thousand years ago, Aesop wrote, "Please all and you will please none."

Whenever you take a stand, you risk the hostility of those who disagree with you. The greatest hero is hated by the forces he opposes. Do you think George Washington was popular in the court of George III? Florence Nightingale had to overcome furious opposition when she entered a profession that "decent women" didn't work at. If you can think of nobody who has reason to dislike you or disagree with you, chances are you haven't recently spoken up for anybody or anything.

The "sweet kid"—liked by all who know her—is likely to be a bland character who has never taken a side, never defended a friend, never tried to right a wrong and never cared enough for anyone or anything to get excited about it. In every crowd, in every community and every school there are plenty of issues worth feeling strongly about—and a few good enemies to have.

7. *Take a wide-screen view of things.* Small children focus

on their own needs and wishes. Part of growing up is a broadening of focus to include the needs and wishes of others. A truly mature person includes the needs of all humanity in his viewpoint.

In a sense, only the baby is a true individualist, being scarcely aware of outside influences and also completely selfish. In growing older, we often have to sacrifice our individuality for the good of family, friends, community, society. An army man must submit to regimentation and order of command to maintain efficiency. A choir girl, for the sake of uniformity, may have to wear an unflattering color or collar. It takes a wide lens to see when the good of the whole is more important than your individual expression. If you understand *why* you are going along, you need not accuse yourself of *thoughtless* conformity.

On another level, the broad view can open your mind to the fact that there are other ways of doing things than the way they are done in your family, in your crowd, in your town. Putting your habits and customs into a broad perspective can help you to examine them and to decide if they are, after all, really meaningful to you.

8. *Help others to understand your point of view.* Though you march to the sound of a different drummer you may not have to be the only out-of-step parader. Perhaps other people would like to tune in on your beat. Why not give them a chance?

For some people, nonconformity is no more than an expression of hostility. If others decided to follow their lead, these people would have to find a new means to break away. But a sincere person who separates from the group or diverges from custom out of honest conviction is usually glad to explain her reasons and pleased if others agree with her. This is really what progress means: one person finds a better way and wins others to his point of view. Why rest content with being merely an individualist when you might also be a reformer?

Ellie's crowd began to turn every party into a lights-out necking session, and Ellie didn't like it. She simply stopped showing up at the parties.

After a while, Bobbi also got fed up. But Bobbi told the other girls how she felt. Most of the girls, once the dissent was aired, admitted that they agreed with Bobbi. They needed just one girl to speak her mind. The next week, the crowd got up a bowling party and lights-out evenings were discontinued.

9. *"I'd rather light a candle than curse the darkness."* Eleanor Roosevelt said it, and the statement points up the difference between positive action and negative protest. If you don't like the way things are going—if you see injustice, hypocrisy, insensitivity, foolishness about you—you can express dissatisfaction by wearing disreputable clothes or singing protest songs. This may help to dissipate some of the anger you feel, but it is unlikely to change any of the things you oppose.

On the other hand, constructive protest—well-thought-out petitions, delegations, applications to student or community government, letters to editors, volunteer work for ideas you believe in—are all reasonable ways to right wrongs and to make society better.

The malcontent, the cynic, the chronic complainer may boost her own ego by sighing or sneering. But the girl who takes appropriate action is expressing herself in the only way that can really help. Next time you find yourself saying, "Isn't it awful?" follow through with the next sentence, "What can I do about it?"

10. *Never stop growing.* Some girls are fossils at sixteen. They won't eat corn pudding because Mother never served it at home. They won't attend a classical concert because they're not used to anything but pop music. They won't listen to a speech by a Democratic candidate because their parents are Republicans.

Girls so set in their ways have little chance of discovering themselves. The mature individual incorporates many interests and experiences. Each stage of life offers special opportunities for growth. Only by being receptive to new ideas and new experiences, by growing *out* as well as growing *up*, can you achieve the individuality of a complete human being.

Make new friends, be alert and curious, read about people and places too remote for first-hand experience. Don't be afraid to ask questions—of yourself and others. One of the most interesting women I know, an anthropologist, recently spent an evening among high school girls in a small town. "They must have been fascinated to hear about your adventures," I said afterward.

"No," said my friend. "Actually, they were apparently so intimidated by my work that they didn't ask me a single question.

They spent the evening telling me about their junior prom. *I* was fascinated."

I couldn't share her amusement. I could only regret that girls who might have learned so much had learned nothing. Don't throw away your opportunities as those girls did. And especially don't hesitate to ask questions or explore new possibilities just because no one else is doing it. Don't catch premature *rigor mortis*. Don't let unreasoned conformity make an automaton of the one and only you.

How Well Do You Handle Your Worries and Fears?

RATE YOURSELF ON THIS WORRY QUIZ	Scared Silly	Jittery	Cool as a Cuke
1. A brand-new date rings your doorbell . . .			
2. You're called in for a job interview . . .			
3. Final exams are coming up . . .			
4. You learn that there is some gossip going around about you . . .			
5. You see the family doctor's car in front of your house when you come home from school . . .			
6. It's a week before the prom; nobody has asked you . . .			
7. The curtain rises on the class play and you're the leading lady . . .			
8. A good-night kiss is getting out of hand . . .			
9. It's time to decide whether to take an out-of-town job or stay home for the summer . . .			
10. Your beau's family is taking you out to dinner at an elegant restaurant . . .			

If all of the quiz situations found you cool as a cucumber, you're simply not for real! Actually, the girl who scored ten Cool as a Cuke's would probably be in more serious emotional trouble than the girl with ten Scared Silly's. Most teen-age girls would be panicked by at least one or two of these situations; almost all would be jittery in every one of them.

Does it surprise you to find that other people are just as frightened as you are? Let me surprise you even more: adults—

those people you think are in such great control over situations—
are frightened too! Even for a fully mature person, it's a rare
day that doesn't turn up some cause for fear, worry or anxiety.
Girls your age are many times more susceptible to these feelings,
primarily because so many of the things that are happening are
new—new experiences, new ideas, new demands, new responsibilities, new privileges and new developments in your bodies.
It would be most unnatural for you to face all this newness with
the calm of an aged philosopher. On the other hand, I'm sure
you'd like to attain some of that ease and serenity as quickly as
possible. Experience will be your best teacher, but meantime,
let's see if we can get a head start by understanding these feelings
of fear, anxiety and worry.

Take from our Worry Quiz the situation that is your particular
bugaboo. Whether you feel most threatened by the exam, the
gossip or the lack of a prom date, here's how you probably react:
your heart pumps harder; your blood rushes away from your
skin, making you look pale; the pupils of your eyes dilate, making
you wide-eyed; and your glands go into overproduction, causing
the sweaty palms, the clammy forehead, the weak knees and the
queasy stomach.

You don't like this fear reaction, but in a situation of real
danger it's a good thing. Imagine that you're walking down a
jungle path and a hungry-looking tiger jumps out of the bushes.
The fear reaction mobilizes you for defense. Psychologists call
it the "fight or flight" preparation. The dilated pupils would help

you see better in the jungle's dim light. Those strong, pounding heartbeats and those glandular secretions would help you run faster than you've ever run before. If you decided to stay and fight, you'd find yourself mightier than you believed possible, far beyond the highest physical fitness rating you ever made. And if the tiger got a scratch in, you'd be surprised at how little you bled—because so much of the blood would have left the surface of your skin.

Of course, you're not likely to meet any tigers outside the zoo. But in our modern society, we still react to danger situations as if they were jungle beasts. And in many situations of real and present danger, these fear reactions continue to help us. It is the fear reactions *without* the real and present danger that you would like to eliminate, or at least put under control. Feeling afraid without knowing exactly why or what you fear is called anxiety. Feeling afraid of something that might happen in the future is called worry. Everybody suffers from a certain amount of anxiety and worry, but teen-agers get an outsize portion. The girl who says, "I feel nervous today and I don't know why," is suffering from anxiety, as is the girl who is restless and irritable or her friend who has "the blues." You're no longer worried about the things that had you biting your fingernails five or six years ago (thunderstorms, perhaps, or large dogs or escalators) but new problems have replaced the old ones.

I would list the five most prevalent teen-age fears as follows:

1. Unpopularity, or the fear of being rejected.

2. Inadequacy, or fear of not living up to your parents' expectations, which often become internalized as your own high standards, particularly about doing well in school.

3. Loss of protection, or fear of separations and responsibilities that come with growing up.

4. Personal changes, or fear of impulses of anger, love, sexual desires, and fear of the challenge of new ideas.

5. New experiences, or fear of being unable to cope with new types of situations.

Fear of pain, punishment, illness and death are common to everybody, though often more acute for girls of your age. The five fears I have listed, however, are likely to be your special "jungle beasts," and the more you understand them, the tamer they will become.

Take your fears about popularity—you see, I assume, that no matter how popular you are, you still worry about being liked and accepted. If you marked down "Scared Silly" for numbers 1, 4 and 6 on the Worry Quiz, you're heavily burdened with fears of rejection. Like a former patient of mine, a high school senior we'll call Linda L.—who was captain of the cheerleaders, in the top fifth of her class in academic achievement, pretty as a pin-up, with plenty of girl friends and a date every Saturday night—you panic over the possibility of not being liked.

"Nobody *really* likes me," Linda told me. "They just put up with me because I'm there." Linda had to learn to like herself before she could believe that other people liked her. Linda's case indicates that The Most Popular Girl is a myth—a label that always belongs to Somebody Else.

Anxiety about marks in school is a different kind of problem. Here, unlike the abstract goal of popularity, you have an actual measure of how well—or how poorly—you are doing. Also, if you are college- or career-minded, grades have a great deal to do with your future success. Still, your anxieties about marks come mostly from fear of disappointing your parents or lowering your prestige among your friends.

Sometimes your parents may expect (or seem to expect) more than you can possibly deliver. Even if the expectation is unreasonable, you are probably upset at falling short of it—almost as if you were a little girl expecting to be punished for misbehaving. As you grow up, it is important to try to evaluate yourself and to decide which demands made on you are reasonable and which are not. If your mother expects straight A's and B work is the best you can do, it's foolish to keep going through anxiety symptoms every time reports come out. If you can't make your mother understand that you're not Madame Curie, ask a teacher or guidance counselor to talk it over with her. Convince her *and* yourself that there are plenty of good colleges with easier require- ments than Wellesley's or Vassar's.

Let me note that some anxiety before exams is a good thing. I don't mean the kind that comes because you've saved all your studying for the night before. A little honest anxiety, however, keys you up to do your best work in much the same way that the "jungle" fear makes you stronger and faster. Too much worrying, though, can have the opposite effect: we all know stories about good students who get overwrought at test time and draw a blank when the papers are handed out. If this should happen to you, tell your teacher and ask to make up the test another day.

Many of your anxieties are less specific and more elusive than those we've just talked about. Going back to that doctor's car parked in front of your house—it is natural to feel concern at this indication that somebody inside is ill. It is also natural to hurry in to see what's the matter. But overreaction—say, to go into a sweat or palpitations (before you learn that the doctor is visiting the family next door)—is not very unusual in girls your age. It reflects a fear for the health and safety of your parents which may stem from mixed feelings of dependence on and annoyance with them. While you say you can hardly wait to grow up and be on your own, part of you wants very much to stay within the security of the nest. Any giant step toward moving away from this security is bound—either consciously or unconsciously—to produce some anxiety symptoms. Your jitters over a job interview or a college application may stem as much from this fear as from a fear of rejection. The first overnight trip on your own, a solo shopping expedition to choose next fall's wardrobe, taking off for a job or a new school—all these ventures into adulthood, while deeply desired, are also deeply feared. It is only small comfort to know that almost everybody feels the same way.

Closely related is the anxiety you feel in boy-girl situations. I'm sure none of you likes to admit that you're afraid of boys.

But what is that uncomfortable reaction you get when your new date is dancing too close or his good-night kiss is going too far? Is your heart pounding and your breath coming too fast? Eyes widening? Palms moistening? Do you wish the ground would open up so you could make a quick disappearance? Well, there's that tiger again, threatening you. But the tiger isn't necessarily your boy friend: you could always ask him to stand back a bit, please. What *is* bothering you is the potentiality for danger in your own mind and body (plus a dash of that fear of rejection). You are developing a set of womanly emotions.

Love, anger and the sex drive are powerful emotions, common to everybody, *not* evil. By recognizing these feelings, by accepting them, you come to use them properly when the time is right. Joanne G. insisted that boys left her cool and unruffled. A blind date ever fazed her and she had no difficulty in either refusing a good-night kiss or cutting off a necking session that she had allowed to go on for a while. "I guess I'm just a cold fish," she told me, rather pleased with herself. After a few talks, she realized what I had suspected all along: she had very deep emotions about contact with boys. But fear had caused her to bury them within herself. So while she showed no symptoms of anxiety on dates, her tensions expressed themselves in other areas, making her so moody and depressed that her mother asked her to see me professionally. Joanne's feelings can be put on the right track and she will become not only a more serene daughter but also a more relaxed date.

It is unhealthy to kid yourself into thinking that you're sexually in neutral. Nor would it be wise to throw yourself into high gear. Try to look at yourself realistically, accept your feelings and control them. This is the way to grow up and to keep those anxieties down to size.

We come now to the question of novelty, the heart of so many of your anxieties. Any new experience is a challenge to your ability to master it. A part in a play, a job interview, a new kind of school assignment are sharply defined new experiences. If they make you nervous, you can understand why. But apart from them, your whole young life is filled with novelty: new people to deal with, new situations to cope with, new attitudes expected from you, new kinds of decisions to make. At no other time in life do so many new things happen so fast. No wonder you feel jittery, self-doubting, irritable, awkward, even panicky at times.

The first speech you make as a member of the debating society will probably be the hardest. The first hour on your sales job in the local five and dime will likely be the scariest. The first morning you spend as a hospital volunteer will be the most awkward. It's too bad that so many of these firsts happen at about the same time, but maybe you can try to spread them out. Remember, though, that awkwardness is not a crime (it can even be charming if not overdone) and that everybody has gone through it. And if you take your mind off your troubles long enough to look around, you'll probably see that most grownups are sympathetic.

These five areas of anxiety don't come near to completing the list. The real world offers us many things to worry about and

our imaginations provide even more. Everybody has tough decisions to make, difficult problems to solve; and there are carry-
overs from childhod that some of us never outgrow. You won't
be able to eliminate fear, anxiety and worry from your life. Even
if you could, it wouldn't be a good idea: the world would never
improve if nobody worried about its imperfections. You wouldn't
be much of a person if you weren't eager to be liked, to live up
to standards, to master situations, to carry out responsibilities
and to fulfill the potential good within you. What you *do* want
to do is cut down your fears to manageable size, to get rid of
the silly ones and perhaps learn to live with those you can't
conquer.

Toward these ends, you might try to apply these seven principles for coping with fears.

1. *Understand that everybody is afraid.* As a teen-ager myself,
I was once deeply impressed when a lovely woman whom I considered the epitome of social grace told me that she was always
afraid of meeting new people and that entering a party made her
weak in the knees. Since that time I've learned that nobody is
immune from social anxieties and that the woman simply knew
herself better than those who are unwilling to admit such fears,
even to themselves.

So it is with most of the fears you suffer. You needn't be
ashamed to show signs of nervousness. You may even find that
once you stop being afraid of being afraid, you won't be quite so
fearful.

2. *Talk about your fears*. In many areas of society, it's considered proper to keep one's emotions to oneself. "Keep a stiff upper lip" and "Grin and bear it" are two expressions that typify this attitude. Actually, it isn't such a good idea. Bottled-up feelings tend to ferment. Talked about, they tend to fall into perspective. It helps to talk about your fears with your friends. It helps even more to talk about them with some understanding adult who can see them objectively. Parents, doctors, religious counselors, teachers or guidance counselors can usually be trusted to hear you out with sympathy and might well come up with some sound advice for easing your worry. Just talking to a disinterested (not *un*interested) grownup can do wonders to clarify your problems.

Have you ever had a problem so complicated that you couldn't face it? Did putting it into words seem to take the mystery out of it? The knottiest problem seems to loosen up when it is discussed reasonably. Furthermore, the act of talking itself releases tension and will probably relieve some of your anxiety symptoms. So *don't* grin and bear it; share it.

3. *Learn techniques for mastering your fears*. If you have ever taken care of a toddler, you've probably been frightened by his *lack* of fear. An eighteen-month-old doesn't know enough to be afraid of moving cars and is likely to wander into a busy street. He would willingly touch red-hot objects and drink poisonous liquids. That's why he needs unwavering attention. Gradually, he learns to be afraid—from often-repeated warnings, from punish-

ments and sometimes from sad experience. Most of your fears were learned in these ways, too. Something that has been learned usually can be unlearned, but it takes work.

You, let us say, have learned never to be bossy because bossy girls are not liked. You learned this lesson out of fear of rejection, just as the toddler learns to keep hands off the stove out of fear of pain. Now you are editor of your school paper, and if you don't start giving some loud and clear orders, there will be nothing to go to press. You are going to have to *un*learn your fear of being bossy or you will fail at your job. First you will think it over; if you're thinking straight, you'll come to question whether the exercising of responsibility really means bossiness. Then you'll find a way to put your orders firmly but pleasantly. After you practice for a while, you should find that you have conquered this particular fear. That's about how it goes.

A number of veteran stage actresses admit that they suffer severe stage fright, not only on an opening night but every time they perform. Nausea, dizziness, "the shakes"—the various symptoms which affect these ladies—haven't stopped them from going on with the show. While they haven't been able to unlearn their fear, they have learned to function despite it. You can do the same thing—but you'll probably find that *your* fear diminishes with each performance because your fears are likely to be less complicated than the deep problem of an actress's stage fright.

In between unlearning and ignoring are other techniques for mastering fears. The girl who's scared of a blind date asks the boy over to her house for dessert and getting acquainted a few days before the big dance. The girl who hesitates to speak up in class writes her ideas on a piece of paper before she raises her hand. One ingenious girl I know once visited a plush restaurant some days before her boy friend's family was to take her there: she felt she'd be more comfortable if it wasn't completely strange to her. And she was right!

4. *Learn to think instead of worry.* While fear and anxiety can be helpful emotions—by keeping you away from danger or leading you to overcome a problem—worry alone seldoms helps you. You tend to worry in circles. Like chewing gum, worry goes round and round without ever getting swallowed and digested. And like chewing gum, worry is habit-forming: the more you indulge in it, the harder it is to break the habit.

But you *can* break the habit by systematically replacing worry with thought and action.

Constructive thinking is very different from worry. Try thinking about a personal problem as you would a problem in arithmetic. First you set it down in clear, workable form and then you think of all the possible solutions, finally choosing the one that seems best. Having made a decision, carry it out. Simple? Not really. Decision-making seldom is, but once you get the hang of it, you'll be on your way to a positive pattern of thought and action.

Remember that worry and anxiety are variations of the fear reactions that prepare your body for "fight or flight." So when you're worried, it's always more healthful to *do* something than to let your tensions churn inwardly.

The shyness and awkwardness that bother you can be relieved by doing something about them. Try developing some physical skills to help you relate to people. Learning to play the guitar, tennis or a decent game of bridge will open the door to easier social contacts.

Some people trying to break the worry habit find that it helps to write down their problems and possible solutions, listing pros and cons on two sides of a folded sheet of paper. You'd be surprised at how many things can clear up once they're down in black and white.

You may find that what you're worrying about is not really the problem at hand but a carryover from other feelings or situations. Such was the case with Kate M., who worried so much about possible traffic accidents that she was unable to drive the car her parents gave her for a graduation present. With some help from her father, she was able to trace back her fear to an accident many years before, a childhood experience she had almost forgotten. Next, she studied accident statistics, finding the odds well in her favor. She took a few extra driving lessons, had safety belts put in the car. In this way, she took to the wheel, converting her worry into positive action.

5. *Develop a philosophy*. The best-laid plans of mice and men —and teen-age girls—often go wrong. A steady beau may change his mind and take back his class ring. The A that you're counting on to get you into the Honor Society may turn out to be a B. Illness and death come, sooner or later, to every family. But we can't live our lives worrying about the worst that can happen.

We try to correct the situations that we can control. Those that we can't control, we try to accept.

Everybody needs a philosophy of life, for both good times and bad. A well-developed philosophy based on the understanding that life can't be an endless highway of smooth driving and fun stopovers helps us to take the bumps a little more easily. Your own religious faith, reading about and discussing the philosophies of other people and your recognition of the fact that the world is not designed to your own specifications should help to give you courage to face trouble.

"Everything happens to me" is a phrase I hear very often from teen-agers. So many teen-age girls seem to feel that they, like the biblical Job, have been especially selected to be stricken with all the world's troubles. Everybody else, they seem to think, lives in blissful happiness while they are hounded by misery. The truth is, of course, that everybody has disappointments, hurts, frustrations and losses, and that nobody is ever unique in unhappiness. Most people have a "public personality" (called persona, from the Latin word for mask) for carrying out their roles and activities. Only when we get to know someone very well do we find the real individual—grappling like ourselves with the problems of living—that exists behind the smiling mask. Recognizing the fact that everybody has problems is the beginning of philosophy.

6. *Size yourself up realistically.* The two-lane road of understanding yourself and accepting yourself leads to the poise and

serenity that most girls wish for. Once you have a fair idea of what you can and can't expect from yourself, you can set reasonable standards physically, academically and socially. A good deal of a teen-ager's difficulties comes from her inability to set such standards, because she simply doesn't know what her limits are. You are still growing. Even when you stop growing physically, you will continue to grow mentally and emotionally. It would perhaps be helpful to recognize the fact that you are in a state of almost constant change, to do the best you can and not to agonize if you can't do better. Within your own standards, you can enjoy feelings of success and achievement denied to people for whom the sky is the limit. No golfing novice would expect to equal the score of a Ben Hogan. No intermediate pianist should fret because she isn't a Van Cliburn. Time is on your side; you have years and years to improve yourself. But some girls at seventeen demand from themselves the aplomb of a woman of forty. Savoir faire doesn't come that quickly, and nobody—except perhaps yourself—expects it of you.

People who set too high goals for themselves are doomed to constant feelings of failure and anxiety. Try to let your goals be steppingstones rather than high mountains. Try to be an individual: self-improvement is fine, but choose a reasonable yardstick to go by.

7. *Keep fit physically.* I know that yours is the age of crash dieting and late-night cramming, but do you know that taking good care of yourself might reduce your jitters, irritability and

mopes? A businessman puts off an important decision until he has had a good night's sleep. How many decisions do you make on too little sleep? Athletes fill up on lean meat and vegetables. But how much activity do you try to accomplish on a between-meals diet?

People who get enough sleep have better control over their emotions (all other things being equal) than people who don't. People who eat well-balanced diets are better able to cope with difficult situations (other things being equal) than people who don't. These facts should convince you that proper rest and diet are important factors in your emotional well-being.

Why not find out what a week of nine-hours-of-sleep-a-night will do for you? And how about applying the suggestions on the Seven Basic Foods chart that's probably posted in your hygiene class? (It might also clear up some skin and weight problems.) Overuse of caffeine and nicotine can make you tense and jumpy. If you are a coffee-drinker, why not try limiting yourself to one or two cups a day? If you are a cigarette-smoker, why are you?

Often, physical illness makes emotional problems. Worries and anxieties loom larger when we're not quite A-OK. When your spirits are dragging and your fears are distressing you, it may be time to see a doctor. And even if all situations seem to be well under control, don't forget your yearly physical examination. Physical health is closely related to mental health. If you want to handle your worries and fears well, keep well.

Your Dreams, Both Day and Night

QUIZ   True   False

1. Dreams can foretell the future.
2. Daydreaming is a waste of time.
3. A person dreams only when she has a problem.
4. Dreams are meaningless.
5. It is harmful to awaken a sleeping person.
6. The analysis of dreams is a recent art.
7. Pipe-dreaming is always a form of escape.
8. A psychologist can find significance in every dream.
9. Girls daydream more about becoming famous than they daydream about boys.
10. Nightmares do nobody any good.

If you answered "false" to every question, you are wide awake to the facts about dreams. Actually, nobody knows *all* of the answers about dreams, but the more you know about the reasons for and the significance of your dreams, the better you will be able to understand yourself. For dreams have their source in ourselves—in our innermost feelings, conflicts and aspirations. Particularly during the teen years, when self-understanding is both very important and very difficult to achieve, you should be using your dreams and daydreams to open doors to self-knowledge.

Dramatic recent studies, in fact, indicate that dreaming is essential to emotional health. The song-writers who advised us to "dream your troubles away" seem to have been on the right psychological track. Since 1960, sleep researchers have been able to recognize dream periods in their sleeping subjects. Most people spend about a quarter of their sleeping time vividly dreaming, though they tend to forget many of their dreams. When research subjects were permitted only nondreaming sleep—that is, they were awakened as soon as they started to dream—they tended to become irritable and restless and to dream *more* the following night, as if to catch up on their dreaming time. So dreaming seems to be a vital function which drains off tensions that accumulate during the day.

Nighttime dreaming may serve as an expression of wish-fulfillment. Suppose somebody has angered you during the day. You go to sleep and dream of vanquishing that "enemy" in a wrestling match. Without that dream satisfaction you might have awakened to a night-long insomnia session of "I should have said . . ." and "Next time, I'll . . ." or, even worse, of tossing about with uncomfortable memories of the insult you suffered. Daydreams afford similar relief. Remember the song of imaginary revenge that Eliza Doolittle sings in *My Fair Lady*? It begins "Just you wait, 'Enry 'Iggins, just you wait!"* and details exactly the sort of wish-fulfillment I'm talking about.

Very often, people have wishes that they don't consciously know they have, which is why dreams and daydreams can actually help you understand yourself better. If you dream and daydream

*Copyright © 1955 by Williamson Music, Inc. Used by permission of T. B. Harms Co.

a great deal about winning the "contest" or running races, there's a good chance that you have many unresolved feelings about competition. Sometimes a dream tries to present "the other side of the picture." If you think that you are deeply in love with Hank and keep having dreams in which Hank is a villain, you can be fairly sure that your true feelings about Hank are somewhat mixed.

It is not usually this simple, however, to understand the meaning of your dreams. For one thing, most people dream in "symbols" and when we are awake we don't usually think in this pictorial way. Let's say that Janice is unkind to Jerry and then feels that, because of her bad mood, he will not ask her to the prom. It is conceivable that she might dream that night of running out on a dock as a ship is pulling away. This dream would be expressing Janice's feeling, "I lost my chance. I missed the boat." Another example of symbolism: Debra had refused to lend her charm bracelet to a good friend. She felt she hadn't, after all, been very big about it. She dreamed later on that she visited a world of giants. In a sense she was saying, "How small I feel!"

I am not recommending that you become a full-time dream analyst, nor that you become overpreoccupied with your own dreams. I do believe, however, that thinking about any recurrent dream situation might help you to know yourself a little better.

Dreams and daydreams are also a source of escape. When the world seems impossible—as it does to everybody now and then—a dream world can be much more agreeable. When your mother says you can't leave the house until your dresser drawers are cleaned out and your father sets a three-minute limit on your telephone calls and your favorite date is seen at the movies with one of the cheerleaders and you can't seem to break the code of your geometry homework—it's quite likely that you'll lapse into daydreams about a carefree summer vacation to come or an even more remote cruise around the world. In fact, such luxurious daydreaming can be the refreshing pause that makes it possible for you to get through the day without screaming or crying.

Night-time dreaming often performs the same function. After a day of things going wrong, you might dream of serenity or triumph and awaken to a mood of happiness and optimism that stays with you long enough to overcome some of yesterday's disappointments.

Dreaming can refresh also by dissipating feelings of fear, anger and frustration. Has a teacher ever lashed out at you for talking in class when the real culprit was the girl in the seat behind you? Possibly speechless with fury, you may have spent an hour or so that night imagining yourself lying close to death in a hospital bed while the teacher, piteously contrite, begged your forgiveness. After this imaginary triumph, you were probably ready to return to school and resume a mature relationship with your teacher.

When your feelings are very strong and there is no socially acceptable way to express them, dreaming and daydreaming are fine channels for draining off the excess emotion. But fantasy is more than a valve for escape and letting off steam; it can serve a positive and constructive purpose: creative thinking. In the business world, brainstorming sessions are based on this type of daydreaming: participants throw in every idea that enters their minds—the whimsical and outlandish along with the more realistic. A notetaker records every idea and when they are all sifted through, there are usually several workable ones which might not have come to the surface if all those imaginations had not gone soaring.

Pure scientists, theoretical mathematicians, explorers, philosophers, all creative persons in any field daydream their way to the paths of discovery. And, of course, everybody with ambition is a bit of a dreamer; for it's the dream of our future that gives us the goals we strive for.

Sometimes your dreams reveal goals you didn't consciously know about. Janet believed that she wanted nothing more than to get through high school, marry the boy she had been going steady with since she was fifteen and settle down to run a home and raise a family. Her school marks were good, her guidance counselor recommended college and her parents encouraged her to go on to state teachers' college. But by the time she reached her senior year in high school, Janet felt ready to announce her engagement, with plans to marry after graduation.

Everything seemed fine, but Janet began to dream of herself attending classes and living in a dormitory. Her daydreams, too, instead of centering upon the wedding, seemed to turn continually to scenes of her teaching a second-grade class.

One night she dreamed that she had misplaced her engagement

ring and was afraid to admit that it was lost. She awakened with anxiety and, because she was a perceptive girl, decided to discuss her dreams and daydreams with the school psychologist.

After a few conversations, Janet came to see what she had been unwilling to face: she did not want to lose Paul but at the same time she really did want to go to college and become a teacher. Once she accepted her conflict, she summoned the courage to talk it over with Paul. Eventually they decided to go ahead with their engagement but to defer wedding plans until Janet had a chance to try college for a year.

All the functions of dreams—escape, letting off steam, wish-fulfillment, self-revelation and thinking out—are functions that answer needs especially dominant in teen-agers. Recent studies indicate that teen-agers are likely to express a certain set of feelings in their fantasies. In general, thirteen- and fourteen-year-olds tend to express anger in their dreams and daydreams. Older teens seem to manifest anxiety: guilt, concern for the future, frustration over disappointments.

Of course your own pattern of daydreaming is as individual as you are. But you might be surprised to see how it compares with the fantasy themes of other girls your age.

Physical attractiveness. In a recent survey of 131 college girls, 95 percent said that they daydream about being physically attractive.

There are ample reasons for this preoccupation. In the early teens, girls tend to be fascinated with their maturing bodies, to compare themselves with their friends and to start thinking about their ideal figure standards. Skin blemishes and awkwardness give rise to "escape" and "wish-fulfillment" fantasies about ugly ducklings who turn into delectable swans.

Older girls, having reached mature physical development, lean toward a "creative" kind of daydreaming in which they imagine the figure they would like to have and very often "dream up" ways (dieting, exercise) for achieving it. The fact is that the further removed your figure is from ideal, the more time you are likely to spend in elaborate daydreams featuring a you with a different body.

Love and sex. There is probably no area of general teen-age concern that causes as much frustration or is as hard to talk about as sex. No wonder, then, that this is a frequent teen-age dream theme. When you were twelve or thirteen, you probably fell in love regularly with a male teacher, a movie star, one of the Beatles—somebody who was unavailable and therefore neither a threat nor a challenge. Gradually, as you took on years and experience, you probably began to dream less fancifully of the unattainable and more realistically of boys you knew and of romantic situations that were possible, if not probable.

Some daydreams serve as a "dress rehearsal": you imagine how you will greet Stephen next Saturday night, what you will say as you step into his car and how you will carry off the evening. This kind of daydream can prepare you for the real thing, even providing you with a poised response when Stephen asks for a good-night kiss.

Sometimes, too, daydreaming about a boy helps to overcome a

fruitless crush. You may find yourself strongly attracted to Richard, who scarcely notices you. Cast as your dream hero, Richard may, after many varied performances, completely work out your interest in him—leaving you ready to turn to a more meaningful relationship with a boy who returns your feelings for him.

Money and possessions. Money and possessions are among our society's most tangible status symbols, and status is what a girl needs to feel when her ego has suffered. When she is feeling put down by the world, she may get temporary comfort by imagining herself driving a sleek convertible car, jetting cross-country for skiing or surfing and, of course, being envied by those who caused her original disgruntlement or disappointment. This daydreaming is pure escape.

For some girls, however, especially those who feel deprived—of love or individuality as well as of material things—dreams of wealth can be real aspirations. These girls are likely to see money as an important goal in life and not only to dream of having it but also to dream up ways of getting it.

Vocational success. Many girls daydream about their futures not so much filled with fame and fortune as with accomplishment and fulfillment of their aptitudes and abilities.

Particularly in junior and senior high school years, when you may feel bored or pressured by academic routine, you are likely to find relief in fantasies about yourself as having *arrived*—in the career and setting of your choice. Right now, many of you are undecided about your future occupations and these fantasies help you to "think through" what it might be like to be a teacher or a radiologist. Furthermore, dreams of independent achievement give you a temporary feeling of freedom in addition to pointing out possible ways for attaining that freedom.

Worry. Not all dreams and daydreams are pleasant escapes or constructive castle-building. Even as wish-fulfillment, a dream can be a nightmare if your wish is to punish yourself. And we can also have nightmares while we are awake—in the form of worry.

The trouble with worry is that it doesn't progress from problem to possible solutions, but goes in repeated circles like a cracked phonograph record. Worry, like all daydreaming, can be habit-forming; but it is unlike other forms of daydreaming in that very little good can come of it.

The way to break the worry habit is to train yourself to work out the real problems that trouble you and to turn off your imaginings about the unreal ones. One of the best methods for turning aside unproductive worry is to involve yourself in a project that requires concentrated thought and action. Bake a cake, clean out your desk or play that game of Concentration you've been promising your kid brother. Doing something to help somebody else is especially effective.

Other common daydreams. Especially attractive to teen-age girls are fantasies of the martyr or suffering heroine and dreams of triumph at great physical or mental feats. The appeal to teens of both these themes should be obvious. As the suffering heroine, you are saying to everyone who has ever rejected you or been unkind or unfair to you, "Aren't you sorry? Now that you see what a truly wonderful person I am, aren't you ashamed that you underestimated me?" In the dream of magnificent performance, you are symbolically casting off all the shackles of inexperience and ineptitude that most teen-agers feel very poignantly. All your shyness and awkwardness disappear as you become the idol of multitudes.

In addition to all these popular dream themes, I'm sure there are a few which are personally your own. Thinking about them in the light of what you have just read, you may be able to understand why they occur to you. There are several ways to use your dreams to help you to grow toward emotional maturity.

1. *Pay attention to them.* It has been said that "A dream uninterpreted is like a letter unread." Too many people ignore their dreams. Though some people claim that they never at all, most of them who honestly try can reconstruct many dreams quite fully.

There is no doubt that dreams are important. Because they are symbolic and involve deep feelings, you will not be able to understand the meaning of each fleeting dream scene. Even psychologists can't always do it. However, recurrent themes and characters and the suggestions of strong feelings are really messages to you. If you think about them, they may help you work out the problems that seem to be, if not on your mind, then very close to the surface.

Thinking about your dreams need not take any more time or concentration than thinking over a conversation you had with your mother or a teacher or a boy you'd like to know better.

One girl I know kept a written record of her daydreams as an experiment. After a month, she noted that she had spent a good deal of her time imagining herself as a corporation executive and sometimes as the first woman judge on the United States Supreme Court. She reasoned that, in these daydreams, she was expressing a need for power and authority. From this, she gained the insight that she was actually tired of being "bossed around" by most of the people she knew. She determined to try to be more healthfully assertive in her relationships, and little by little she got over the habit of being a permanent "yes-girl."

2. *Gain the knowledge that conquers superstition.* One of the best ways to vanquish fear is to face it and analyze what it really is that we are afraid of. Despite the normal reaction of wanting to forget about nightmares, psychologists know that recurrent bad dreams are the ones that usually point out areas of unresolved conflict. Therefore, recurrent nightmares are the ones that call loudly for attention.

A high school junior we'll call Nancy kept dreaming that she was a thief. Over and over she would suffer the mortification of being arrested, tried and sentenced to jail. The dream, in variations, came most frequently during weeks when she had school examinations. "What is it that I am stealing?" she asked herself.

She was an excellent student, usually got top marks and never cheated.

It came to Nancy's mind, after much thinking, that it was *time* she had been stealing, from her studying—an evening out with a girl friend, an hour of reading for fun—and this was making her feel like a thief. Imagine feeling guilty over a few hours away from schoolbooks! She began to understand how hard on herself she had become, how afraid that she wasn't trying hard enough. This insight helped her to feel less competitive about her marks and to find more satisfactions outside of being the best student in the class.

Nightmares are very often highly dramatized and bizarre over-statements; daydreams also tend to exaggerate. A feeling of anger is translated into great violence, a trifling annoyance is blown up into epic injustice. A mild physical attraction evolves into a day-dream of passionate love. Once you understand the tendency of dreams to be highly colored expressions of rather ordinary feelings, you will be less frightened of them. You can be more objective when you know that the gigantic fantasy of a lion is just a shadow image of a kitten.

3. *Treasure your dreams of glory.* Daydreams are most con-structive when they help us translate fantasy into reality. Many great acting careers are rooted in daydreams of taking center stage and bowing to applause. Dreams of fame and glory, of helping others, of expressing your talents or making your parents and friends proud of you—these are the stars to which you hitch your

wagon. If your dream is bright enough and steady enough, and if you have the determination to plan and the vigor to work hard for it, you are very likely to approach that star—near enough to enjoy its warmth, if not actually to grab hold of it.

4. *Don't get lost in dreams.* Put your dreams to work as goals and then put yourself to work attaining those goals. The girl who dreams of being beautiful while biting her nails or nibbling candy is actually working against herself. Instead, she ought to do something to make herself the beauty of her dreams. With skin care, proper diet, well-cut clothes and a flattering hairdo, there will probably be enough real compliments and real satisfaction to make the daydreams less compelling.

Similarly, a girl who does a lot of dreaming about becoming a teacher though her parents cannot afford to send her to college should inquire about scholarships and part-time work rather than lose herself in unprofitable fantasy. Here and now is where and when we operate, and if we dream ourselves out of it too often, it's a sure sign that something is going wrong. You should get enough satisfaction from the life you lead to keep daydreaming in its place as a pastime and not a permanent occupation.

Helen went through one of those long, unexplainable dateless periods. She took to going alone to the movies on weekend nights and spending the rest of the time in an intricate fantasy relationship with a man more charming than any of the boys who didn't call her. After several weeks of this pattern, Helen was invited to a party. She actually refused the invitation, preferring the comfort of her daydream to the anxiety of meeting a lot of new boys.

When you wrap a daydream around you like a warm blanket, trying to protect yourself from a cold world, it's time to stop and think. Are you becoming a daydream addict, reacting to every difficulty with Instant Fantasy? If you spend most of your energy daydreaming, there is little left for real accomplishment and the discovery of satisfaction in real life.

5. *Don't feel guilty about daydreams.* As I have said, dreams are often tremendous exaggerations of real feelings. And they are an escape from real inhibitions and constrictions. Some of the things you are likely to do in your daydreams will almost inevitably be things you would never do in real life. If you work out your anger by daydreaming of beating your father over the head with a stick, how much better this is than being rude to him at the dinner table. Once your anger is "dreamed away," you may be able to tell him quite reasonably what is bothering you and he need never know about the bump on the head you gave him during the afternoon fantasy session. By working off your anger you actually helped rather than hurt your father, and there is no reason to feel guilty about it.

Similarly, daydreams about sex are likely to carry you beyond the bounds of convention and propriety. Why feel guilty about them? In the safe world of fantasy you have worked off emotions that might be extremely troublesome on a date with Ricky. You are responsible only for your actions; your thoughts should be free to explore, to escape restrictions and even to warn you of possible consequences of acting out some of the things you think about.

6. *Remember that great doers are great dreamers.* Never to dream or daydream is as unhealthy as living entirely in a world of fantasy. Life without dreams is dull indeed, lacking romance and imagination, goals and vision. The nondreamer inches his way around a daily routine without adventure and without inspiration.

By keeping your feet on the ground and your eye on a star, you can learn to maintain the vital balance between your needs and desires and your obligations and responsibilities to yourself and to others. Dreaming and doing are two weights on the scale. The proper balance is yours to discover and to work with in your own way.

You and the Dragon Jealousy!

"I just don't know what the boys see in Betty."

"My kid brother is a spoiled brat."

"Johnny can't make the state scholarship and I think it's a waste of time for him to try."

"Marcy is impossible since she got her own car."

"I wouldn't want to be in that crowd. They're a bunch of cats."

The common basis for all these remarks is one complex emotion: jealousy. Jealousy is responsible for much of the malice in our world. Though it is not necessarily green-eyed, it is indeed a monster, feeding on insecurity, breeding hostility. Hardly anyone is immune to an occasional scratching of the monster's claws and many people are all but consumed in its jaws.

Teen-agers are particularly succulent morsels for this monster. If you think about it honestly and carefully, you'll probably find that jealousy—in one of its various disguises—is behind some of your actions.

There are plenty of reasons. For one thing, as your relationships grow away from your family and toward your friends, you are increasingly concerned with how you stack up against your contemporaries. For another, you are beginning to wonder where you will fit in the world and, until you find yourself, you will tend to be somewhat discontented. Self-acceptance is at the opposite end of the pole from jealousy. Right now, you are only beginning to visualize the "self" you want to be. Until you achieve it—or make peace with the "self" you are able to achieve—you'll probably find sprouts of envy shooting out in all directions.

"I wish I had Janey's figure." "Oh, what I'd give for Ellen's brains." "Why can't I be . . . ?" "Why don't I have . . . ?" These are common teen-age phrases; sometimes they are spoken, sometimes just thought and sometimes unconsciously at the root of many of your actions. What *causes* all this discontent and what can you do to tame the monster?

Understand first that jealousy exists to some degree within everyone, and, like most complex feelings, it's not all bad. If you use it constructively, it can be a spur to help you improve yourself. We all need to have heroes or ideals on whom to model ourselves. When "positive" jealousy of Janey's figure starts you working on your own unhealthy eating patterns, when admiration of a teacher's vocabulary sets you to building your own word power, then you are putting your emotions to excellent use. Jealousy *needn't* turn to malice; it *can* foster ambition. Many successful people find motivation for hard work and self-discipline in their longing to achieve the accomplishments and rewards of other people. Dissatisfaction with ourselves or our nation or our surroundings often leads us to strive for better things.

That same dissatisfaction, however, can express itself in hatred, self-pity, bitterness or cynicism. Envy as a destructive, dangerous force can sour friendships, wreck relationships, spoil family life and really poison a personality. Just think how much of our literature—from the Cain and Abel story to *Othello* to *Snow White* —deals with the ravages of jealousy on its victims and *their* victims. Think, from your own experiences, of the harmful gossip, the cruel digs, the slights and the hurts that are caused by jealousy.

What lies at the basis of jealousy? Fear of loss, longing for affection, and hostile emotions. Anyone who possesses something that you fear you don't have ("What has she got that I haven't got?") can become a target for this kind of envy. Most teen-agers' jealousy, however, is primarily directed toward brothers or sisters, girl friends and boy friends.

Envy of brothers and sisters. Hard as it is to avoid envying a brother or sister, it's even harder to recognize this envy because it assumes many disguises. Usually, a teen-ager feels that she doesn't like her sibling simply because he's not pleasant. You're ashamed of your younger sister because she's noisy and messy. You think your parents give in to her too much. You're annoyed with your brother because he invades your privacy. In most instances, these feelings are a mask to cover up real feelings of rivalry that have not been honestly confronted.

Rivalry is a natural part of growing up with sisters and brothers. As a baby, you are the center of your universe, completely dependent upon your parents' care and very much the object of their attention. When a baby brother or sister is born, you are forced to share the attention. If you don't actually get relegated to second place, you certainly have to share first place with a younger child who is even more dependent than you are. He continues to be a rival as he goes through his cute toddler period while you are perhaps a gawky in-betweener, looking on as he gets the cuddles and the compliments. Similarly, if you have an older brother or sister, you are likely to resent his or her privileges and achievements. When you reach your teens, many of those old negative feelings still smolder in the ash heap of your memory. When fanned by a minor conflict, they can flame into a major conflagration. Right now—while you are so engrossed in discovering who you are and what you can do—you are particularly sensitive to sibling annoyances.

Envy of girl friends. It's almost impossible to avoid at some time or other being jealous of girl friends, even your *best* friend —a terribly uncomfortable feeling, which usually involves a great deal of guilt and self-deception. Some girls envy a friend's popularity or good marks; other friendships sail smoothly until the friend gets pinned or is taken on a vacation to Europe or moves into a grand new house. On the one hand, you feel that you ought to bask in your friend's good fortune. On the other hand, you wonder, "Why her and not me?" The closer your friend is —and the more beloved—the more you may resent achievements or bounties that seem to separate her from you.

People are susceptible to jealousy in individual ways. Each of us tends to envy in others that which we feel we can't ever have ourselves. If you are shy, you will probably be attracted to —and ultimately be jealous of—a friend who deals easily with people and social situations. If you're just average in schoolwork, you might well be proud to be the friend of the class "brain," but the very qualities you admire may turn into the objects of your envy.

Sometimes jealousy even becomes chronic, develops a pattern.

Here's what happened to Ellen, a girl with lots of friends, good marks, plenty of dates. Every time she began really getting close to a girl friend, something seemed to happen to spoil the budding friendship. She was smart enough to see that something was wrong with her if she couldn't sustain a close relationship. She thought it out as objectively as she could and came to see what the trouble was. Since early childhood, she had been pushed by her parents to fulfill very difficult goals of scholarly and social success. If she brought home a B mark, her mother's typical comment was, "Is that the best you can do? I'll bet Joanie got an A." If she came home from play looking untidy, her mother might say, "Why is it that Gwen always stays so neat?" Her parents were always anxiously concerned with her friends' accomplishments and forever comparing them with Ellen's. With her girl friends held up as standards of achievement, Ellen started to see life as a competitive struggle. Every triumph for a girl friend seemed to be a setback for herself.

When she recognized and understood her competitive motivations, Ellen was able to set her *own* standards and take joy from her friends' accomplishments. Though she couldn't eliminate *all* pangs of jealousy, the monster lost most of its power to control her behavior.

Jealousy of a boy friend. This is quite a different kind of jealousy. You're not likely to begrudge a boy friend his looks or his luxuries, his personality or his achievements. You are more likely to be jealous of his attentions.

A certain amount of possessiveness is quite natural. But when it becomes excessive, it often brings on the very thing you fear most: loss of the possession. This kind of jealousy is particularly dangerous because it usually comes on only when you really like the boy. The pattern is that the more you like him, the less you allow him his freedom of friends and interests. What could be more destructive than jealousy that keeps a boy from studying, from enjoying his own friends and hobbies, from developing his talents, from becoming the very man that you ought to want him to be?

Yet many girls expect to be paid constant court, to the detriment of the boy's schoolwork and outside obligations. Wouldn't it show more genuine, less selfish love if a girl were concerned more with her boy friend's happiness than with her own pride?

Closely related is jealousy over a boy friend's interest in other girls. I realize there's a lot of competition about dating and there's probably not a girl in the world who *wants* to share her special boy with others. But extreme jealousy can be a big problem.

Janie spotted her Bill talking with great interest to a pretty girl she'd never seen before. Suddenly, she was green with envy. She held it in until her date with Bill that evening, which she started off with sulking silence. Bill wanted to know what was wrong and late in the evening, she tearfully told him. Bill laughingly said that the girl was his neighbor's niece, in for the day from her home upstate. He added that she wasn't very bright.

Reassured, Janie was happy again and Bill was flattered that she cared about him enough to be jealous. For the rest of that evening he was especially tender and solicitous of her. But the incident started a progression of similar ones. Whenever Janie felt that Bill was a little less attentive than usual, she found a reason to vent her jealousy. These incidents grew in frequency and intensity until Bill, no longer flattered, became resentful. He began to foresee a lifetime on Janie's leash and he asked for his pin back.

A healthy boy wants companionship, sympathy, affection and loyalty. He *doesn't* want—and shouldn't have—a millstone around his neck. The healthy girl wants a whole boy, not a pet poodle.

If you examine your motives when you find yourself getting jealous of your boy friend's time and interests, you'll probably find that your feelings arise from your own sense of insecurity and fear of losing something valuable to you.

In fairy tales, Prince Charming always rides up to kill the monster. But life is no fairy tale, and there *is* no sure method to squelch your own envy. There are, however, a few good ways to keep it under control.

1. *Admit that you're jealous.* Many people are too proud to admit—especially to themselves—any grave flaws in their personality. Jealousy, after all, is a pretty ugly word. But jealousy is a normal emotion. Most people live with it; it's what you *do* with it that counts.

Once you face your jealousy, it often loses its power. Like

many a monster, it cowers back into its cave when you stand right up to it.

When you start finding fault with your friends, when you pick silly fights with your kid sister, when you suddenly and unreasonably decide that your boy friend is neglecting you or sneer at his efforts to win recognition for himself—it's time to put your pride aside and *face* the jealousy behind it.

2. Enjoy yourself. The happier you are, the less jealous you are likely to be. Self-pity and self-blame are jealousy's cohorts. If you can accept yourself, you are less likely to be angry at those who shine in areas where you are weak. If you set impossibly high standards for yourself in all areas, you will come to think of yourself as inadequate and very probably be jealous of those who seem more successful than you.

In short, if you like yourself, you are less likely to envy others.

Self-satisfaction, however, is not the natural state of the teenage years. Nor should it be. You haven't had enough time or experience to learn what you can and can't achieve. But you can start in the right direction by recognizing your assets. When you're all wrapped up in feelings of self-pity or inadequacy, you tend to dwell on your weak points and forget your strong ones. Your assets seem unimportant compared with the liabilities you're worrying about.

If you'll take the time to sit down and draw up a balance sheet, you might be surprised at the results. List all your good points, your possessions, your endowments, your aptitudes and achievements on one side. List your weak points, or the things you feel deprived of, on the other. Then—and this is most important of all—mark a star after every liability you think you can improve or correct.

Now, did you include *all* the assets? Good health? Reasonably good family relations? Straight, even teeth? A facility at the piano? The name of a true friend? A nature that is compassionate or curious? And I do hope you were able to include a sense of humor.

Now—are you as bankrupt as you thought? Probably far from it!

Use your assets and enjoy them. *Improve* your liabilities where possible.

3. *Work for what you want.* Learn to harness your jealousy and use it to work toward realistic goals for yourself. There are enormous untapped resources within you; most people just roll along like a twelve-cylinder engine using only half its power.

When you find yourself jealous of someone, pinpoint what it is that you envy in her. You could probably develop the same facility or trait in yourself if you were really willing to work hard at it.

Phyllis is a natural athlete; you are naturally clumsy. Is admiration at the pool or on the courts worth your taking tennis lessons or joining a swimming class at the Y?

Paula has knockout clothes; your wardrobe comes more slowly, and from bargain racks. Do you want good clothes badly enough to get a job and earn the money for them? Or to take up home sewing and make your own wardrobe? Or to trim down your figure till clothes look wonderful on you?

Getting what you want usually takes a lot of time and effort. The editor of the school paper didn't just fall into the office one day. The class beauty probably attends conscientiously to her figure, posture and grooming. You may not be able to outdo or even match these girls, but you can come closer to your ideal if you work at it.

4. *Understand that the world is not your private oyster.* Many so-called adults believe in the childish notion that the world exists to satisfy them. Such people cannot escape ultimate disillusionment. And when the blow falls, they are usually deeply jealous of the unscathed people around them.

If you don't expect the moon on a silver platter, you will not be disappointed when it doesn't arrive.

More specifically, how often do you expect much more than can be reasonably given to you? You can't be invited to *all* the parties. You are never going to get *everyone* to love you. You can't be in *every* clique or part of *every* activity. You can't be good at *everything*.

Most people who develop a pattern of chronic jealousy try to keep up with a standard that exists only in their imaginations. When their demands—of themselves and others—are not promptly or easily met, they decide that the world is a cruel, cold place.

Most reasonably happy people expect very little to be given to them. They feel the world owes them nothing and anything good that happens is cause for joy.

An attitude of "What can I do to make my world happier?" instead of "What did the world do for me today?" can go a long way in fending off destructive envy.

5. *Look outside your little circle.* Jealousy thrives on smallness of mind and outlook. Recent studies were conducted in Antarctica of men who were forced to live together in close quarters deprived of outside contacts and interests. Energy without channels for outlet soon turned to hostility among these men and a great variety and depth of jealousy resulted. Adventurers and scientists who would ordinarily be above such pettiness squabbled over the ownership of a cake of soap, the placement of an ashtray, the loyalty of friends.

It's always in small, somewhat isolated groups—such as an exclusive clique or a camp cabin or a school club—that jealousy seems to find its angriest expression. This suggests that one good way to avoid problems with jealousy is to maintain a wide circle of friends and a wide area of interests.

If your crowd seems to be rocking with competition and cattiness instead of the latest hit record, maybe it's time you opened your doors to new members and new projects. Local hospitals are usually eager for volunteer workers. How about working on Christmas presents for underprivileged children? If you're jealous of Carol, whose parents are whisking her off to Florida for

Christmas vacation, you can spend the two weeks feeling miserable, or you can develop some other friendships or some accomplishments of your own.

People who are busy are seldom jealous.

6. *Take a look at the other side.* When you're jealous of a girl friend, you tend to overvalue everything she has. You forget that she has problems of her own, just as worrisome to her as yours are to you. In our culture, where cheerfulness is considered a virtue, most people manage to cover up their feelings of sadness and insecurity with a smiling veneer.

The story goes that the gods were once awakened by the moaning and groaning of people, each complaining about the weight of his particular package of troubles. To keep them quiet, the gods allowed everyone to exchange packages. The people happily took over one another's packages of troubles and the gods went back to sleep—only to be reawakened by the same people, now clamoring to have their old, familiar packages back again. Think about your package of troubles and then think—realistically—about the package of the girl you envy most. Would you really want to trade with her?

7. *Learn to wait for your rewards.* As we grow older, our needs become much more complicated, and the time between desire and fulfillment increases. A baby is hungry; he cries; his mother gives him a bottle. But a man may hunger for a career as a doctor. It takes him about ten years of schooling, internship and residency before he is able to practice medicine. If, during this period, he

resents every high school friend who gets a good job and is able to marry and have children, he is going to be a very unhappy man.

If you keep your sights trained on a goal of your own, you're less likely to feel competitive with or jealous of girls who gather their rewards before you get yours. If you have your eye on admission to a top college, you'll probably have to sacrifice a lot of playtime in favor of study. It doesn't make sense for you to be jealous of other girls' time for fun and games.

The same goes for a freshman who wants to be leading lady in the senior class play. The sensible approach is to join the drama club, work hard at the parts you're given and patiently wait for your own opportunity. Even if you don't make the lead when you're a senior, you will have had lots of fun, gained solid acting experience and perhaps learned the joys of being a constructive part of a group.

If the sacrifices seem too hard for you and you find that you cannot banish your angry envy of other girls' enterprises, perhaps you ought to change goals.

8. *Cast a warm eye*. Every once in a while, it's a good idea to detach ourselves from the bustle of the here and now and take a farsighted look at the human situation. If we can see—from an astronaut's-eye view—what little people even the greatest of us are, we may be less prone to hurt one another through jealousy or any of its ramifications.

In the long view, does it really make much difference if a

friend has more dates than you do, if a parent seems to dote upon the baby of the family, if your boy friend chooses to bowl with the boys on Wednesday nights? In the long view, the qualities which are important are love and compassion, kindness and co-operation. You may see, if you look as from afar, that your individual achievement of your individual goals matters more than competition with others, that your development as a fully realized, responsible person has very little to do with what other people accomplish or possess.

How To Cope With Inferiority Feelings

"Betsy always exaggerates. She probably has an _____ _____"

"Bill never looks anyone straight in the eye. He's shy because of an _____ _____"

"My parents think Jeff is rude, but I tell them it's just his _____ _____"

"Jane won't go on a blind date. She says she doesn't want to spend an evening with a creep, but I think she has an _____ _____"

"Milly never volunteers an answer in class. In fact, she never volunteers to do anything. It must be an _____ _____"

"Joan acts like a snob, but she says she can't be friendly because of an _____ _____"

"Sally is an awful flirt and always has to be the life of the party. Could she have an _____ _____"

Fill in the phrase "inferiority complex" at the end of each of the sentences above and you'll get some idea of the range of this overused, often misunderstood term.

Inferiority feelings are common among teen-agers and might well be at the root of the behavior described in all the quotations above. Though teen-agers aren't the only people troubled with inferiority feelings, you are especially vulnerable to them. For as you begin to feel your way toward a place in the world, you tend to look for a handy yardstick by which to measure yourself. You are, in effect, leaving your secure place in the family and jockeying for position among your friends; so your friends become the likeliest yardstick. Comparing yourself with other girls *has* to leave you with some feeling of "not measuring up." How *could* you be as pretty as, as bright as, as popular as, as athletic as, as talented as, as poised as the prettiest, brightest, most popular, most athletic, most talented and most polished girls you know?

Even if you have already learned that nobody gets all the winning tickets, you're likely to expect or want more than you have. It's hard to be realistic in a world where movie and TV heroines wake up mornings with every hair in place and nary a wrinkle in a dainty nightgown. You see photographs of teen-age models in clothes that fit to perfection and you read interviews with clever young women who seem never to suffer the slightest feeling of awkwardness. Many of you haven't seen enough of real life to recognize the falsity of these "public images." Make-up men and wardrobe women follow the actress around her movie or TV set, combing and pressing before every shot. Models' clothes are pinned to fit that way and even the models can't sit down in them. And most of the clever young women are flanked by even cleverer publicity men. Nobody is that perfect and it's no wonder that girls who think in terms of public images invariably fall short of their ideals.

Realistic ideals are slow and difficult to come by. How many teen-agers have a clear idea of what they want to be and to do in life? More important, how many can estimate the possibilities opened by their own talents and aptitudes? During these years of exploration, it's almost impossible—and probably not even desirable—to specify the life you want to live, the person you want to be. So you may try different roles, grope in many different directions, and your weaknesses are exposed. Until you hit upon your areas of strength and superiority—and work out goals that use them—you will probably feel inferior in many of your endeavors.

Often teen-agers' feelings of inadequacy are aggravated by the gap between what they are and their parents' dreams of what they should be. Sometimes mothers and fathers have entirely different dreams for you: your father may be pushing you toward the Honor Society while all Mother wants is for you to be the Sophia Loren of the senior class. Whether or not your parents harp on it, the knowledge that you don't measure up to your parents' expectations can gnaw great chunks out of your self-esteem.

So it's not surprising, then, if you feel inferior to some of your friends, many adults you admire, your parents' dream-teen or the person you yourself would like to be. But inferiority feelings do not always stop at recognition of weakness or incompetence. Sometimes they wear a mask of bravado or aloofness. The girl with the permanent cool, the show-off, the clown and the Personality Queen are all possibly harboring even deeper feelings of inadequacy than the girl who doesn't need to try so hard to disguise them. Certain symptoms indicate the presence of inferiority feelings: the avoidance of new people and new situations; a tendency to embarrass easily; a need to boast and act superior; supersensitivity to any kind of criticism; and sometimes apathy, as if you're thinking, "I'm not going to do it well anyway, so why bother to do it at all?"

But whether her feelings are simple or complex, even the most confident of teen-age girls often finds her self-esteem vulnerable in at least one of the following areas.

The girl in the mirror. Many of you spend hours examining your mirror image, keeping up with your fascinating transformation from girl to woman. With all this concentration on the physical, it's only natural to exaggerate details: a pimple becomes a major catastrophe, an irregularity in the profile puts you in line for casting as one of the three witches in *Macbeth,* two pounds overweight and you're waiting to be enlisted as fat lady in the circus. The small-breasted girl feels as humiliated as her friend who considers herself grotesquely overdeveloped. Many teenagers dread gym class because they are embarrassed to change clothes in front of their classmates, sometimes feeling emotionally —as well as physically—exposed. This overemphasis on physical characteristics often leaves everyone feeling less beautiful than everyone else.

Baubles, bangles and beads. In our materialistic society, many of you base feelings of confidence on possessions. Girls who haven't so many clothes in their closets or rooms in their houses as some of their friends have are often troubled by feelings of inferiority. Swimming pools, cars and country club memberships are—I think you will agree—absolutely unreliable guides to character and personality yet many girls use affluence as the measuring stick by which to assess themselves. Since there is almost always somebody around whose father makes—or spends —more money than yours, you are bound to feel inferior if you use this standard of comparison.

The honors list. As more and more American teen-agers go to college, the competition for grades gets keener. In the old days, "beautiful but dumb" was considered a compliment, at least by the donor. Now a girl who is an average student may feel like a complete dud. Many of you who are not *quite* on top feel that you're scraping bottom.

Yet, as most of you are well aware, school marks are not always the most accurate measure of mental ability. And in the years beyond your school days, many other qualities will count at least as much toward success as the ability to get good grades.

The woman of the world. Teen-age girls generally believe that there is something disgraceful about being young, inexperienced, timid and ingenuous. Some of you feel inferior because you lack the polish and aplomb of older women or even of some of your friends who have "been around" more than you.

Onstage. Meeting new people can draw out feelings of inferiority that you didn't know you had. Many girls see life as a popularity contest and "making people like you" becomes very competitive.

Everybody in Middletown knows Rita as Dr. Wilson's daughter, the girl from the big house on Grove Street, the sister of last year's track captain, the daughter of the president of the Women's Club. Around Middletown, Rita has plenty of poise. But when she takes a summer job in a distant town and no longer enjoys the "instant identity" of her family, she suddenly finds a need to promote herself, to describe her family's position in Middletown. She is not at ease; she doesn't listen to other people because she is too busy thinking up ways to let them know who she is. In fact, she goes through many of the symptoms of inferiority feelings.

Gerri is a different case. She has never lived in one community long enough for her family to become established. "New people" are almost the only kind of people she encounters. Basically, she is no less attractive than Rita, but she sells herself short. As a habitual "outsider," she feels that everyone else is "in." To every girl she meets, she attributes remarkable endowments of beauty, charm, cleverness and suavity. Labeling herself a born loser, she doesn't bother to join the game. She is sloppy about her hair and clothes and when she enters a conversation, she comes on apologetic and self-abasing.

Both Gerri and Rita need to learn that, in new relationships, everyone starts at Go. Rita, in depending upon family position to make her acceptable, puts herself down as much as Gerri does by thinking everybody is "in" except her. When they discover that there are no insiders and outsiders but just people, they may worry less about their own imagined inferiority.

The same lesson holds true for dating. When you're worrying over what your date is thinking about you and what your crowd will think about your date, you're bound to be insecure. The best solution is to forget about the impression you're making, and find out what you think about the boy you're with.

Other matters that can be troubling are poor athletic ability, speech defects, a physical handicap. Family problems, too—a father who drinks too much, divorced parents, a problem sibling —can bring out serious doubts about your *own* adequacy. If it is your nature to feel comfortable with yourself, you will be able to overcome personal or circumstantial handicaps and to assess yourself reasonably. But if you're "inferiority-prone," almost any characteristic can become a focal point for self-contempt. And if you "look down on" yourself, most people will accept you at your own assessment.

What makes some of you so hard on yourselves? Why does one girl suffer agonies over defects she would readily accept in other people? Why is she so full of self-doubt while her friends, who are very much like her in other respects, are reasonably at ease with themselves and their faults?

The strangling vines of inferiority are usually rooted in child-hood situations. The first chance we have to see ourselves as others see us is in early childhood. If your parents have treated you as if you didn't measure up, you are very likely to see yourself in that light. We are all born helpless and unless we are allowed to enjoy achievements as we grow up, we cannot grow in self-esteem. If a parent does everything for a child, the child is likely 'o be unprepared to do things for herself and to agree with her mother's repeated observation: "You can't do anything right." Some parents permit their children to do too little; others force them to try too hard. In schoolwork or conduct, parents may expect more than a child is up to, and even when their feeling is unspoken, the child is usually painfully aware of the fact that she has displeased or disappointed them. Deprived of the joy of achievement or the taste of success, a child begins to see herself as a failure. Many a girl comes home with a silver medal only to be told by her disappointed father, "Well, maybe next time you'll get the gold one."

Parents who are themselves extremely successful or who represent themselves as infallible can also be hard on their child's self-respect. A girl who grows up hearing her father's work glorified or being told, "I hope you'll be half as beautiful (or charming or clever) as your mother," may develop serious doubts about her ability to measure up to her parents.

Even more often, inferiority feelings can be traced to an exceptional or extremely competitive brother or sister. Having robbed an older sibling of his starring role in the family saga, a younger sister may feel his anger as constant criticism, bullying and one-upping that takes the bloom off her achievements. Or she may be outshone by an exceptionally bright or attractive younger sibling. Few phrases are more deflating than "Even your little brother does it better than you."

But even with wise parents who emphasize the individual merits of all their children and who appreciate each for what he is, some people will find themselves inferiority-prone. Some of us just seem to be perfectionists; and since nobody achieves perfection, the perfectionist is doomed to feelings of failure.

Regardless of the sources or the extent of your inferiority feelings, and whether they are chronic or just occasional, you can help yourself to relieve them. No one I know of *any* age *always* feels equal to *all* people and *all* situations, but the following formula will provide a pick-me-up when you're feeling put down.

1. *Pinpoint your problem.* When you find yourself either bowing to or overcompensating for feelings of inadequacy, call your behavior by its name and ask yourself some questions: What situations cause me to feel inferior? What do I feel inferior about? To whom? Why?

Greta found that she tightened up at parties. Visualizing the scenes that made her feel inadequate, she pictured herself getting along fine with the boys until the other girls began watching her critically and exchanging whispers about her. She knew this picture was not taken from life and she tried to figure out where it came from.

She found an answer. Greta is the youngest of four daughters. Their mother was a practical nurse, often out working, and the older sisters had taken over Greta's upbringing. Greta remembered scenes when she had been playing with friends while her sisters looked on, often correcting and embarrassing her. Now in her teens, with two of the sisters married and one in college, Greta was still carrying out her childhood pattern of resenting girls who "looked in on her." At parties, her friends became her "supervisors" and, as in childhood, made her feel inept and inferior.

Once she realized this, Greta could remind herself that her girl friends bore no resemblance to her sisters, and she would be less prone to bring past emotions into present party situations.

2. *Chalk up your assets.* Once you pinpoint the areas in which you feel inferior, you're bound to be left with others in which you don't. If you concentrate on developing your good points, you'll be less likely to brood over your weak spots. Rather than compete against other people's skills and gifts, discover your own and learn to use them. When you think in terms of assets and liabilities, you'll find that everyone has a goodly assortment of both.

3. *Do; don't stew.* Improve your weak points. You're clumsy on the dance floor? Take a course in modern dance or rhythmic exercise to tone your muscles and enhance your grace. If you feel inferior because of the way you look, start with a really good haircut and styling, adopt a sensible diet plus generous helpings of exercise and fresh air. Almost everyone can raise her scholastic average by working harder on schoolwork; can increase her date schedule by getting around and meeting new people; and can get money for new clothes by babysitting or taking a part-time job.

4. *Sight your targets.* One of the troubles with inferiority feelings is that they discourage you from trying very hard. If you

see yourself as a loser, you usually don't even bother to enter the contest. Without entering, you *can't* lose, but you can't win either.

The perfectionist sets her goals too high while the defeatist sets no goals at all. Neither can enjoy success and the confidence that comes with it. To strive to be better than we are is part of our cultural heritage. The girl who gives up before she starts—or drops out as soon as the going gets rough—only reinforces her low opinion of herself.

The right idea is to work toward a goal, but to choose that goal carefully. If you're going to make a dress, don't pick the most intricate pattern in the book and then tear it up because you're not Coco Chanel. Start with one of the simplest patterns and when you have mastered it, go on to more difficult ones.

The first time you're on skis, it is foolish to expect to ski like your instructor. Just to learn to walk on your skis is goal enough for the first day. Step-by-step progress may not be dramatic, but it can be very satisfying. When you learn to ski down a molehill, congratulate yourself. In a few years, with good instruction and plenty of practice, you will probably be able to ski down a mountain. But if you consider every spill a failure and no small achievement good enough, you'll be too discouraged to go on.

5. *Talk out your feelings with a good listener.* If your feelings of inferiority are chronic and painful, get someone to help you. A talk with an understanding adult, a favorite aunt, a guidance counselor, a clergyman or a psychologist can help you clarify

your thinking and gain the insights of someone who has un-doubtedly had similar feelings to cope with. Just talking about your feelings often brings them down to size. Furthermore, talk tends to dissipate tension and you may find that a half-hour's conversation leaves you feeling a great deal more at peace with yourself.

6. *Reward your achievements.* Promise yourself a night at the movies after you've finished your book report. When you have taken on a job—volunteered for a class committee or been assigned to clean out your dresser drawers—and have done it well, reward yourself with a new lipstick or a pretty ribbon for your hair; enjoy being good to yourself. Dare yourself to join a choir or an arts-and-crafts group—any new activity you have a taste for—and reward your courage with a beauty parlor appoint-ment or a book you've been wanting to read. Drive yourself to produce the best term paper or oral English report that you've ever done or to lose five pounds or to learn to play tennis or to give a party and—mission accomplished—present yourself with a personal gift.

7. *Measure up the most successful girl you know.* Instead of comparing yourself with all the "lucky" girls, choose the girl you admire *most* and hold her up to the same yardstick that you use for yourself.

I think you'll learn two important things: first, that the object of your admiration doesn't measure up in every category; second, that your yardstick is a tyrant. Perhaps, after this experiment, you'll take off the pink-tinted glasses you use for looking at other people and the black-tinted ones through which you look at yourself. If you can see yourself and other people through the same clear eyes, you'll probably find that you're not so far beneath the others as you've been telling yourself.

8. *Take a change of scene.* The girl who had a hard time learning to read and was labeled "slow" in the first grade may continue through school believing herself to have low intelligence. On changing schools in the seventh grade, this same girl may be tested and shown to have a far-above-average intelligence. Her label changed, she now becomes a top student.

This is not an uncommon situation, and it illustrates the damage that labels can do, for we do tend to see ourselves as others see us and others tend to see us as they saw us the first time.

Rhoda had been a chubby child, and although at sixteen she was of average weight, she continued to think of herself as fat and clumsy. Her schoolmates remembered her as the fat, unhappy outsider of kindergarten days. Family friends invited her to spend spring vacation at their house in a distant city, and there she met people who saw only the teen-age Rhoda. They liked her. She went to parties with boys who had never heard her called "fat, fat, the water rat," and her happy manner reflected the attractive girl they all saw. Rhoda returned home with enough self-confidence to help change her image there too.

Everyone benefits from a change of scene and perspective. If you can't wangle an invitation to travel, you can join a regional club, take a summer job away from home or offer to spend a vacation as "mother's helper" to an older cousin who will help you meet new people.

If you feel inferior to your friends, you might also consider a change of crowd. If you are the poor girl in a rich crowd, the bookworm in a party-girl crowd, the slow girl in a fast crowd, you may begin to feel inferior though all you are is different. A girl of average height can feel like a midget if all her friends are over five feet nine. In a group of oddballs, it's the evenball who is odd.

I would not advise anyone to associate *only* with people who are like her, but I do think it's a good idea to seek your own level in some of your friendships. Everyone needs friends who appreciate and enjoy her and who can share her interests.

9. *Remember the hare and the tortoise.* It is a long, winding road from the helplessness of infancy to the competence of maturity. No one expects you to have the polish of a woman twice your age. If you try to leap the track from novice to expert, you are likely to find that other girls, who took their time gathering experience and expertise, have gained the confidence that you are only pretending to have. Maturation is a slow process. Accept and enjoy your youth and it will lead you, quite naturally, to the maturity you admire.

10. *Map your own voyage.* The destination that brings the glow of success to one girl may be just another spot on the map for someone else. All of us have our Golden Cities and they are not the same place.

Jane wants to be a professional dancer. She goes to class three times a week, practices for hours on the other days, and she is becoming very good. But there is no point to your feeling "less excellent" than Jane. After all, you don't expect to be a ballerina.

When you discover the talent or ability that you want to cultivate, let us hope that you will work at it with proportionate effort. The trick is to do what you can do and like to do, to do it well and to enjoy it.

Discovering and developing your special talents and interests is one of the biggest projects of your teen years. The girl who learns to excell at even one thing has a fine booster shot against the inferiority virus. For in the end, it's the fulfillment of your own abilities that makes your achievement as good as the best in the world.

All About Anger

Alice had the highest marks in English in the senior class. Traditionally, the student with the best marks was asked to read the class poem at commencement, but the head of the English department asked Alice if she would mind letting Alvin read the poem since his average was almost the same and he had a much stronger voice. Alice agreed readily and calmly explained the teacher's reasoning to her disappointed parents. That night she had such a severe headache that her doctor ordered a sedative.

Betty went on a double date with her best friend, who concentrated her attention on Betty's boy friend. Toward the end of the evening, Betty accidentally spilled a bottle of ketchup over her friend's escort.

Carol visited a great-aunt who was convalescing from an operation at a local nursing home. She noticed that most of the people there were very old, had no visitors, and seemed to have nothing to do but sit numbly in a drab lounge room. At the next meeting of her club, she urged the girls to work up a musical program and perform at nearby nursing homes and Golden Age Clubs.

What do these girls have in common?
All of them were angry.
Anger is a basic human emotion, one which finds its expression in many different—and often mystifying—ways. All of us live in a state of changing balance between the creative forces of love and pleasure on the one side and the destructive forces of hate and anger on the other.

The slow march of civilization has been directed toward the

control and appropriate channeling of our destructive forces and the affirmation of the constructive side of our nature. Anger, as an expression of destructive feeling, can be a deeply disturbing emotion, and that is why it is often disguised—sometimes almost beyond recognition. If, however, you want to understand yourself and others, it is important to know when and why you are angry.

Just as your body temperature rises when you have a physical infection, your anger rises when you meet a psychological obstacle. The common physical signs of anger—flushing, increased respiration, tightening of the muscles—indicate that your body is mobilizing for action. The kind of action you take—whether you fight to overcome the obstacle, indulge in a temper tantrum or crying fit, or turn your anger against an easy target rather than your immediate adversary—depends as much on your personality as on the circumstance.

Every stage of life has its peculiar "anger-provokers." You are not likely, as is your baby sister, to throw a tantrum because your mother won't put chocolate in your milk or to be as disturbed as your father when a candidate he believes in fails to win a senatorial nomination. Teen-agers are likely to be angered by partiality on the part of parents and teachers, bossiness or disloyalty in friends, the thwarting of plans, other people's hostility and ridicule. Sensitivity in these areas shouldn't be hard to understand. Moving from the child's world of happy endings, good guys and bad guys and share-and-share-alike into the competitive adult world of subtle shadings and degrees and not always just rewards, the teen-ager can scarcely avoid a sense of outrage at broken illusions. When a parent proves fallible or a friend disloyal, the cry goes out: "Unfair! Unfair!" And in that cry is gathered up a teen's rage at seeing once again that the universe is not designed to please her.

Bossing by parents and friends is another strong irritant. Here you are, beginning to feel and act upon your independence; and there they are, trying to "control" you. If you were still a child, you would expect to follow orders. If you were completely grown-up, you would feel free to ignore them. But most teen-agers still feel a good deal of conflict about when and when not to take direction and therefore greatly resent the "bossiness" that arouses these doubts.

As the center of authority shifts from parents to the "crowd," a domineering friend can be just as irksome as an oversolicitous parent. But the greatest source of anger among friends is disloyalty: friendships reach an acme of importance at your age, but they also tend to be transitory. Today's best friend may be tomorrow's enemy; today's confidante, tomorrow's tattletale; today's charmer, tomorrow's baiter. The shifting allegiances of teen-agers raise dark clouds of anger.

It will hardly surprise you to learn that frustrations about boy friends and dating plans are common teen-age nettlers. Rejection by a boy you like or a crowd you want to join may infuriate you only slightly more than rainfall on the day of your barbecue or a virus on the eve of a class dance. Sometimes everything seems to happen all at once, making a girl so irritable that a hint of hostility—from parent, friend or teacher—is an invitation to battle. In other words, your anger may be lying there in wait for a chance to erupt.

One of the greatest provocations to teen-agers is ridicule. To be laughed at, slighted or put down seems to be the crowning insult. The insecure person finds it very hard to be a good sport, and few teen-agers are so sure of themselves that they don't mind being made fun of. The ones who mind it most and respond most angrily, however, are usually the ones who get the most teasing; a girl who can laugh at herself doesn't make a good target.

One sign of approaching maturity is a change in the *objects* of your anger. Your mother says, "Better take an umbrella," and you're suddenly clear-minded enough to reply: "You're right, Mom. It does look like rain." Your boy friend announces that he can't make a Coke date because he has to mow the lawn for his father and you are able to excuse him agreeably. Your girl friends laugh when they learn that you've joined a madrigal group and you can laugh with them, perhaps rejoining with "There's no accounting for tastes!"

As you grow older, the things that make you angry are often less personal, more abstract: cheating, lying, bigotry, unethical business practices, war and its waste of life, poverty and its waste of human potential. When you cry, "Unfair!" you're as likely to be attacking social injustice as individual disappointment.

With maturity, the grounds for protest widen to include humanity's problems as well as personal annoyances, and your anger might well lead to action to help ameliorate some of these problems.

Anger, however, doesn't always manifest itself in constructive action. Such channeling requires the addition of reason to emotion. In its simplest form, anger without benefit of reason is expressed when a two-year-old tries to destroy something that has hurt him: he'll smash a toy on which he has stubbed a toe; he'll fling from the table a bowl of soup that doesn't taste good to him; he'll hit a playmate. The age of literally hitting back is long behind you. Since earliest childhood, your parents and your society have taught you *not* to express anger directly. You have been told in many ways, "Girls don't fight" and "Nice people don't yell." Depending upon your background, aggressive behavior may have brought on punishment, cost you a friend or caused so much unhappiness that you were overwhelmed with guilt. The "ladylike" image that most little girls are led to acquire doesn't permit much free expression of anger, so you have probably developed other ways of coping with frustrations and irritants.

Rebellion. Though it's usually parents against whom teen-agers rebel, disobedience toward teachers and civil officials, the breaking of rules and protesting against conventions also fall into this category.

At the end of one of those weeks when everything has gone wrong, Judy finds herself in gym class and, somehow, furious at her instructor. The teacher begins warm-ups and Judy moans loudly, "Not kneebends *again!*" Through most of gym period, she makes herself as obtrusive and objectionable as possible until, playing basketball, she accuses the teacher of calling an unfair foul against her. Judy's unreasonable behavior stems from the whole week's frustrations.

Very often rebellion is negative: Maria hands in an assignment late or not at all; Bobbi "forgets" her promise to be home by midnight; Kathy neglects to make her bed on her mother's bridge day; Joanne's marks fall far below her ability; Edie "loses" the music she was to prepare for her piano lesson—all may be indirectly expressing anger.

It is healthy to rebel against unreasonable or unfair authority, but chronic defiance against *all* authority is a sign that perhaps *you* are the unreasonable party.

Gossip. Talking over a party—past or future—speculating about a new girl in town or recounting amusing experiences with friends makes pleasant conversation; Lori can't be accused of gossiping when she tells about Diane's losing a shoe at a band concert or Sue's finding a great bargain at a dress sale. But too often the talk takes a malicious turn: speculation subtly becomes denigration; character analysis becomes character assassination; the humorous anecdote becomes ridicule. People who indulge in this kind of gossip seldom realize how much anger they are expressing. More often than not, gossip is idle anger that has become focused on a convenient target.

Loss of temper. Swearing and obscene language—just because they are socially unacceptable—are by-products of anger. A tantrum can help discharge some of your stored-up hostility. However, it seldom brings forth a constructive solution to the problem that caused it.

Sherry had a tantrum when her parents refused to give her a new dress for a party. Her parents got tired of her tears and shouting; instead of trying to sooth her, they simply left the room, closing the door behind them. Doubly infuriated, Sherry grabbed an apple pie she had just baked (in a glass pie plate) and crashed it to the floor. Nothing happened. An hour later she was still alone in the kitchen, sheepishly picking up squashed apples and broken glass. Result: she paid for a new pie plate, baked a new pie and still didn't get the new dress she'd wanted.

Ellen lost her temper during an agrument with her brother. At the peak of her pique, in what is accurately described as blind fury, she spilled her brother's goldfish bowl. Taking a cue from her behavior, he emptied a bottle of ink over her just-finished term paper. Result: two scared goldfish and about six hours of retyping.

When you lose your temper, you usually lose your argument, for the other people involved have a choice of ignoring you or retaliating in kind. When you fling reason aside, you invite them to do likewise.

The silent treatment. The long sulk, the frigid snub, the stubborn silence make up a tantrum in reverse. They, too, do little to help your cause.

Liz owes you a dollar, and rather than go through the embarrassment of asking for it, you simply cut Liz when you pass her in the hall. If Liz is well on her way to maturity, she may catch up with you and ask, "Is anything wrong?" But if she retaliates with more silence or if you refuse to tell her why you're angry, you will lose not only the dollar she has forgotten about, but also her friendship.

Sulking resentment toward a teacher or employer who has annoyed you leaves him in the dark as to your complaint and can freeze you out of a comfortable relationship.

Competitiveness. Some girls feel they have to win every event; they are not content to be runner-up in any category. Anger is usually the source of such high-tide ambition. The racer sees herself as worthless if not a winner and looks at all other people as her rivals.

As a child, Tammy was repeatedly told she was clumsy and shy. Angry at her deficiencies and at other people for failing to accept her, she gradually built up a compulsion to "show them" by being best at everything. If a friend got a new dress, Tammy bought a more expensive one. When the girls compared Christmas presents, Tammy's had to be the most lavish (even if she had to exaggerate). She was so intent on getting top marks that she frequently copied other people's test answers. In athletic contests and in the drama club, she butted her way to the lead. Tell a joke and Tammy topped it; describe a good-looking date and Tammy had a handsomer one, who was also brilliant. Tammy turned every conversation into a challenge and, needing to be the winner, she actually came out the loser. Competition can be fun, but most people prefer to compete in sports arenas and few like to be forced into contests.

Ambition or competitiveness can help you to achieve your goals. But unharnessed as an expression of anger, it is more likely to defeat you and destroy your relationships.

Direct action. A slap at an annoying mosquito is a fine example of direct action against the cause of anger. Human situations, however, seldom permit the luxury of direct retaliation. As I pointed out earlier, one of childhood's first civilizing lessons is that it is dangerous to try to destroy an offender. Mature people find it relatively easy to voice complaints against offending friends or colleagues, to change a routine that has become frustrating, to eliminate various annoyances from their lives. There are, however, problems without answers and puzzles without solutions. When you find that your fight against City Hall becomes a solitary game of hitting your head against its stone façade, direct your attention elsewhere: a spirited game of tennis, an exhausting bike ride can help discharge angry energy while you accept the fact that there are some obstacles that you cannot overcome.

The most important thing for you to know about anger is that it *must* be expressed. Have you ever tried opening a pressure cooker before the steam has had a chance to escape? If so, you have probably witnessed an explosion—food splattered over the kitchen walls and ceiling. People, like pressure cookers, can generate a great deal of heat, the pressure of which—if steam is not let off—can cause a blow-up. Most psychologists agree that unexpressed anger does not just "go away." The impulse will find a way out, usually a more troublesome one than a simple response would have been.

Many girls, particularly in our polite society, have learned to feel guilty about or afraid of anger. If a temperamental outburst brought on childhood punishment, then was anger not dangerous? If disobedience made your mother feel bad, didn't it make you feel guilty? If "nice" girls were gentle and passive, wouldn't aggressive behavior mark you "bad"? Homes in which anger is unacceptable often produce children who cannot accept their anger. This doesn't mean that they're any less angry than other people, but just that their anger is repressed. Depression, anxiety, the unexplained black mood are ways in which a person takes her unconscious anger out on herself. Sometimes the anger explodes as physical symptoms—headaches, skin eruptions, various illnesses which seem to have no purely medical diagnosis.

Displaced anger. Anger can also be deflected from its real target and focused on a person, an object or an idea that seems safer. This displacement can explain the fury you feel toward your younger sister shortly after your date has called in sick, the hard time you give your mother after you've been rebuked by a teacher. You may not feel free to talk back to a teacher or blow up at a boy friend, but family members make handy targets, like the "whipping boys" employed by oldtime monarchs.

Another handy target for displaced anger is the scapegoat, he who gets stoned to express a whole community's hostility. The scapegoat can be an unpopular individual, a minority group or an abstraction like "the Communists" or "the Establishment." Research shows that as a community's level of frustration rises (because of unemployment, a heat wave, even poor garbage collection), so the tendency also rises to use a minority group as a scapegoat. As conditions improve, the scapegoating diminishes. A similar curve can apply to individuals: when things are going well in your life, you are likely to think well of other people. If you find yourself picking on somebody, better consider what you are *really* angry at.

Anger can be your master or it can be at least a part-time servant. Turning your anger, when possible, into a tool for growth requires first the will to do so, then a good deal of self-understanding seasoned with enlightened self-control.

If you choose to master your anger rather than let it master you, the following suggestions should help you to approach that goal.

1. *Don't bury the hatchet in your own back.* Your first step is to admit that you are angry, even if only to yourself. Once you recognize your anger, you can consciously choose your way of expressing it. You might decide that the satisfaction of a quarrel is well worth the possible repercussions. You might decide to ignore an insult until the insulter needs a favor from you. Or you might conclude that you got what you asked for. What you do with your anger is not so important—psychologically speaking—as your knowing that what you feel is anger.

Many teen-age girls have special difficulty in handling their anger with their parents. It is often difficult to admit hostility toward someone you love; yet it is impossible to grow up without occasionally feeling furious at the most loving mother, the kindest, most generous father. Parental love can be a great obstacle to a girl who desires independence, and obstacles bring on anger. Permit yourself to feel angry at your parents, to learn that love and anger are not mutually exclusive, and to search for ways to alleviate the causes of your anger.

2. *"When angry, count ten before you speak; if very angry, a hundred."* The statement is Thomas Jefferson's but the idea is even more applicable today. In Jefferson's time, you'd have to take a pretty long walk to tell a neighbor off in his living room, and there was no danger of a statesman's outrage exploding before television cameras. The age of speed makes it even more imperative to think before you act in anger.

Our first angry reactions are seldom the ones we pursue in the light of reason. Many people withdraw from a heated scene until they calm down enough to regain equilibrium. Others, fired with anger, write letters to the offender but hold off mailing until the next day. Seldom are the letters mailed. There are, in fact, very few situations in which a pause between impulse and action can be harmful; in most cases it will prevent embarrassment or regret.

3. *Don't let "the wind of anger" blow out "the lamp of your mind."* Anger wants a target; angry people look for somebody to blame. Often, in the heat of anger or from their unconscious needs, they blame someone who has little or nothing to do with

the rage they feel. Sometimes they blame themselves for situations beyond their control. Most frequently, those who lash out at the whole world are in reality angry at themselves.

If you hope to reach mature self-understanding, one of your chief challenges is to look objectively at the target of your anger and to recognize the difference between villain and scapegoat.

4. *Try to uncover the cause of your anger.* The object of anger is not always the cause. You're angry with Bonnie because she was five minutes late for your meeting at the library. But Bonnie has been tardier at other times (and probably you have been too) and it didn't bother you nearly so much.

If you find yourself unusually irritable, overreacting to petty annoyances, more than customarily apt to find fault or disagree, there is probably something you want and are not getting or something you don't want and are getting too much of.

Once you begin to look for the underlying cause of your anger, it may be fairly easy to come upon. Perhaps an older sister is planning a wedding and taking over your share of your parents' attention. Maybe your school schedule is too heavy for comfort. Possibly you're dissatisfied with the quality or quantity of dates you've been having. It is surprising how many possible causes of anger come to mind once you begin to think about it.

Sometimes, however, the real cause of your anger remains a mystery. In this case, it's advisable to talk it over with a guidance counselor, a close family friend or trained psychologist. For without finding the cause, there is little hope of a cure.

5. *Talking can help.* If you have been hurt by a friend's careless words or disappointed by an inconsiderate boy friend, explain your feelings to the offender. "You know, Mary, that I'm sensitive about my weight. I wish you wouldn't bring it up in public." Or "I think you should have called if you were going to be late, Don." Such reasonable registrations of your point of view will probably bring on a sincere apology.

If, on a more complicated level, your anger is roused by a pattern of living that collides with your changing needs, you may have to do a lot more talking. Perhaps you will have to point out to your parents that you need more privacy—that you resent their opening your mail or entering your room without knocking, that you want to choose your wardrobe without your mother's assistance or to entertain a date in the living room without your parents' presence. Calm discussion is likely to win more concessions than sulking or curtness. Your mature approach may even help to convince them that you are indeed growing up and less in need of supervision.

6. *Learn from experience.* If you are at all aware of yourself and your surroundings, you have already learned that certain people and certain situations make you angry. The sensible thing to do, then, is to avoid them. Why continue to spend time with a girl whose constant gossip about all her other friends leaves you angrily wondering what she tells *them* about *you?* Why keep dating a boy whose showing off annoys you? If you hate to visit a certain aunt and uncle who run a marathon quarrel, why not

send your regrets next time your parents go there? If you are irritated by the pettiness and indirection of club meetings, why attend them? There are plenty of unpleasant people and situations that cannot be avoided. By skipping those that can, you will be lowering your anger level and possibly making the others more bearable.

Experience may have also pinpointed many things that you say and do which make *other* people angry. If you are alert and considerate, you will learn after one or two mistakes to avoid people's sore spots and to tread very lightly when danger signals are lit.

7. *Work it off: bake a cake, take a walk, wash the dog.* There is not always a solution to a problem or an appropriate way to express anger. When you find yourself angry and cannot express your feeling without hurting someone or losing your own self-respect, you can at least discharge your rage harmlessly.

Since your body is mobilized for a fight, some vigorous exercise is in order. This is a good time to scrub a floor, take a long walk at a brisk pace, paint a splashy picture, pound some clay or dance to wild music—all of which can serve to restore your sense of humor as well as your emotional balance. Pour yourself into a project, and if it's a constructive one—a cake for the family, a bath for the dog, washing the car for your father— you may feel even better than you did before you got angry.

8. *Will it be important in 1990?* It helps to remember how rapidly feelings and situations change. The party you weren't

invited to will fade someday into distant memory. The test you failed will become, if remembered at all, simply a low point in your high school history. The mortifying boner you pulled will be a funny story to tell at a future party. Taking a long view can dilute momentary fury. Taking an objective look at yourself and your situation can prevent your overreacting to petty annoyances.

9. *Make your actions count.* "Isn't it awful?" is a popular game among high school girls. "Isn't it awful," goes the chorus, "that half the class cheats on the honor system?" And "Isn't it terrible that our town has no place for teen-agers to get together after school hours?" And "Isn't it too bad that nobody has befriended the foreign exchange student?" How often have you played "Isn't it awful?" without even thinking of taking action to improve the situation?

Compassionate people react with anger to conditions that seem unfair, but, although many feel called upon to voice their complaints, few feel chosen to do something to improve those conditions. "I'm just one person," goes the apology. "One person can't do anything."

Actually, all groups are composed of many "just one persons." And when you pick up a banner to take individual action, you may find a great many others ready to join you.

If you are disturbed by cheating but appalled by tattling, why not consult with a group of like-minded classmates and petition for a change in the ineffective "honor system"? If you want a teen-age canteen, why not get up a delegation to solicit help from community organizations or town officials? If you're unhappy about the reception of a foreign student, why not be the first to plan a party for him?

When you feel strongly about a political or social issue, write letters to your congressman. Most legislators are sensitive to mail from constituents. Join a political party; work for a cause you believe in; protest against cruelty and injustice as strongly as you can. (Remember, though, to try to differentiate between well-grounded anger and random hostility looking for an outlet.) Using conscious anger to make the world a better place is the healthiest kind of self-expression.

10. *"Anger is one of the sinews of the soul."* In an essay written in 1642 Thomas Fuller noted that the man who feels no anger has "a maimed mind." There is, indeed, something sick about people who are unable to work up a strong case of anger at anything—a kind of emotional flabbiness that permits them to be passive onlookers at crime and inequity.

To dismiss injustice with a shrug, to accept cruelty, dishonesty, narrow-mindedness as "the way of the world," is to minimize human nature. To feel no outrage at the outrageous is to minimize your own humanity.

Anger should be a "muscular" emotion, giving you the strength to fight against evil as you see it. As a dynamic force in the struggle toward a better world, anger has no equal. Great art, great reforms, great acts of charity are motivated by man's anger against obstacles to human welfare. If you want to be a contributing member of the human race, rather than an apathetic hanger-on, keep your anger in fighting trim.

Like fear, anger tends to be magnified in dark, secret places. Brought out into the open, it can be either dissipated harmlessly or used to great advantage.

As William Blake wrote in 1794:

> *I was angry with my friend:*
> *I told my wrath, my wrath did end.*
> *I was angry with my foe:*
> *I told it not, my wrath did grow.*

The Question of Conscience

Somebody turns out the lights at a party. You don't know your date very well but the others are necking and you don't want to appear "cold," so you join in.

Your mother gives you her prized necklace to wear on a special date. You wear it out of the house, then take it off because you don't really like it.

You know your brother needs the family car, but your parents don't know it. You arrive home first, get permission to take the car, hurry off before before your brother gets home.

Your parents want you to be a fine piano player and they pay a lot for the lessons. Whenever they go out for an evening, you spend your practice hour plunking the guitar.

You double-date with your best friend and find her date more attractive than your own. You concentrate on him all evening, and within two days he calls you for a date.

Your teacher leaves the room during a test, asking the class to put itself on the honor system. A friend asks to look at your answer sheet; you hand it over.

Your feelings about the situations above will vary in degree from the feelings of every other girl who considers them. They are not so much a question of right and wrong as a matter of individual response.

Almost all of you feel guilty from time to time. Some of you spend most of your days under a cloud of vague, uncomfortable oppression which—at bottom—is also a guilt feeling. It is important to understand that guilt is a normal emotion, that a conscience is standard operating equipment. Some people have stripped-down sports car models, geared for high speed and high adventure—fun while the running lasts, but dangerous and not recommended for the long pull. Others have solid gold limousine consciences, which assure driving comfort and the admiration of bystanders but are too cumbersome for free movement. Ideally, your conscience should be tailored to the life-roads you travel. But in reality, nobody can choose: your conscience is determined by such factors as the upbringing your parents gave you, your religious training, your friends, the society you live in—and, I hope, your own thinking.

No two people have identical standards of right and wrong, nor do they experience guilt in exactly the same way. A girl's conscience is as distinctively her own as are her fingerprints.

A healthy conscience acts as a friendly local policeman. When you start to veer away from your own sense of "the right thing," the inner policeman holds up a hand, gives you a warning or a talking to and perhaps a small fine. You learn from the experience and resolve to do better next time.

A weak conscience creates confusion and disorder in a personality. A girl whose inner policeman is sleeping on duty often finds that when he finally wakes up, she is in deep emotional trouble.

Equally unhealthy, the too strict conscience is oppressive, insensitive to human needs and frailties, quick to punish for the most trivial infringements. Instead of the friendly policeman, there is a tyrannical gestapo which inflicts a variety of punishments: depression, self-contempt, a sense of inferiority. Guilt can also make you physically ill or bring on a tendency to accidents. Whatever the means, the end is always self-punishment.

During the teen years, your conscience gets a real workout. Questions of right and wrong come up more often than before. The rapid changes in your body, the upsurge of sexual interest, the pressures toward college or career, the pull away from parents and the newly complex relationships with friends all combine to make this a guilt-producing period.

Some of the most common problem areas are the following:

Growing away from parents. It is almost inevitable that feelings of guilt will color your relationship with your parents. For one thing, there is usually a tension between parents' expectations and teen-agers' ability or desire to meet them. If your father's ideal daughter is someone quite different from you, you may feel guilty about being unable to fill the gap. Or you may respond with anger or rebellion to a parent who tries to fit you into an uncomfortable mold, and *then* feel guilty for going against him. Disagreements with parents are often a losing proposition: if you don't get your way, you're bound to have unkind thoughts about them or do unkind things to them—which eventually makes you feel guilty. If you do get your way, you may feel just as guilty for having disappointed them. Underneath all the open conflict, there is often the uncomfortable feeling of disloyalty. Your interests are moving away from the family and your dependency is gradually lessening: you may become conscious of the fact that your parents care more about you than you care about them.

To a sensitive girl with loving but possessive parents, the situation can be poignant indeed. And almost no girl goes through her teens without some tugging at the leash and without some guilt feelings because of it.

Lying. At what point does a fib turn into a blatant lie? This is a question that bothers most teen-agers. Should you be strictly honest and tell your father that in your opinion his new suit already looks old hat? Should you spare your mother worry by telling her that you're going to a movie instead of to a roadhouse? Is it easier to tell Paul that you can't go out because you have a headache than to say truthfully that you simply don't want to? What do you do when Betty asks you to say she spent the night at your house? And what do you—or don't you—tell Evelyn when her steady calls you for a date? Questions like these come up often in everyone's life and answers that don't satisfy your conscience are likely to stir it to reprisal.

Sexual feelings and masturbation. Most girls feel torn with doubt and guilt over their curiosity about sex and their expression of sexual feelings. The fun of dating can be completely overshadowed with worry about how far is too far. Alone, many girls experiment with their own bodies and find that, afterward, they feel guilty and ashamed. Some girls feel guilty just because they are maturing and are becoming interested in sex. While they may be *doing* nothing about it, their consciences don't permit them to *think* about sex with impunity.

Anger. Most girls have no trouble getting angry with somebody or something far removed from them, but anger toward someone with whom they have close ties often produces strong guilt feelings. It doesn't always make a difference whether you blow up at your mother when she insists on an early curfew or react passively and seethe inside. The guilt feelings still follow. During these years, when parents' *don'ts* so often conflict with girls' *wants,* the anger-to-tension-to-guilt pattern is almost inevitable.

Success. Sometimes you feel as if you're completely hopeless: you wonder how anybody—besides your parents, who *have* to— could like you. And then, not so long afterward, you may feel exactly the opposite: how can anybody be as lucky as you? Your face and figure are okay; your marks are good; you have attractive clothes and live comfortably; you have girl friends and boy friends; all's right with the world. But is it? It's just at a top-of-the-world time like this that you suddenly begin to think about the unfortunate girls you know and about misfortune in general. Thinking about the misery and poverty of others, you start feeling guilty about your own well-being. Why am I so blessed? What did I do to deserve this? And then, very often: something terrible is going to happen to me in order to even things out.

A fall from the heights is a favorite theme in literature and mythology. The furies come to pursue those who luxuriate in their own good fortune. An oversized conscience invites the furies, and guilt can take all the joy out of achievement, sometimes even keep people from trying to better themselves. It's important to learn to live comfortably with your assets as well as your liabilities.

Some of you must also learn to accept success. Whenever there's a winner, there is also a loser. If you worked hard for your prize, you may feel guilty for having been so competitive. If you didn't, you may feel unworthy of it. But the winner of a scholarship or the lead in a school play has no more cause to feel guilty than the girl who is gifted with beautiful features or has the advantage of a rich father. All advantages can be used in constructive ways. When they are, nobody need be ashamed of having them.

The group. As you grow older, your friends' opinions become increasingly important—until you are mature enough to stand on your own. A little girl needs the approval of her parents. At seventeen, she also needs the approval of her peers. Group opinion may become so important that you sometimes act against your conscience in order to go along with the crowd. Then there is conflict: the pressure of public opinion may make you feel guilty if you buck it, but you probably feel even worse if you join in activities that you personally judge to be wrong. It's hard even for adults to maintain the delicate balance between personal standards and group fashions. For teen-agers, it's harder. Probably there will be times when you lose your balance.

Just as there are valid and invalid reasons for feeling guilty, there are healthy and unhealthy ways to cope with it.

Few of you, if questioned, would reply that you think cheating in school is honest or right. But how many of you do cheat, with the excuse that "everybody's doing it"? Matters of conscience, however, go deeper than fashion, and "everybody's doing it" is often unsuccessful at beating off guilt feelings. Furthermore, investigation almost always shows that there are not so many "everybodies" as you might think. A little smoke doesn't necessarily indicate a gigantic fire; rumors are not statistics. What a few—or even many—other people are doing should not affect your own standards.

Another unhealthy way to cope with guilt is to decide to send your conscience on vacation or—what is more likely—to leave your conscience at home while *you* take the vacation. Take for example Martha W. During the summer before her senior year, she and some girl friends rented a beach cottage for two weeks. Martha packed swimsuits, shifts, toothbrush and hair spray, but she intentionally left her conscience behind. This one time, she told herself, she was going to cut loose. At the beach, with boys she expected never to see again, she was a Martha that the hometown boys wouldn't have recognized.

Back at home, though she believed that her escapade would remain secret, she gradually slipped into a depression. She lost interest in her friends and her schoolwork, and life seemed bleak and ominous. Only after psychological counseling was she able to settle her "nerves" and recognize that her conscience had been a stowaway on her trip.

The girl who tries to drown her conscience in alcohol or to evade it by telling herself, "Just once won't hurt," is making the same mistake. Guilt feelings may wait in the background while the cheater goes after her prize or the flirt steals her friend's boy friend, but when the mission is accomplished, they usually come forward.

The historic excuse for unkind or dishonest action is "They deserve it, anyway." Another rationale is "She did it to me, so I'll do it to her." From there, it's only a small step to "She'd do it to me if she had the chance, so I'll do it to her first." Wars begin on such faulty reasoning. So do widening circles of irresponsible behavior. A stalwart conscience is not so easily deceived.

Finally, some young people set themselves above morality. They feel that they are in some way special and don't need to follow the rules. Some take license from feelings of dissatisfaction with the way adults run the world. Some honestly think that they can attain freedom and individuality only by ignoring their ethical and moral strictures.

Certainly there are flaws in the "establishment"—plenty of them. There are often wide gaps between public ideals and private practice. Some of our society's traditions are outmoded. I hope that all of you will make yourselves aware of these problems and do something about them. But constructive rebellion is the outcome of hard thought; mindless rebellion is just an easy way to get around your conscience.

As for the me-first philosophies, they work well for people who live alone, on desert islands or in ivory towers. Living among others, your own best interests are served when you are concerned with other people's needs as well as yours. If one person tosses an orange peel from a car window, the street doesn't become a garbage heap. But if everybody littered, our roads would be both ugly and impassable. Just so, one infringement of the rules doesn't matter much in the grand scheme of things. But general lawbreaking would bring on chaos. Who should be the one who is allowed to toss the orange peel?

Obviously, we must each take the responsibility *not* to do the thing which, if generally practiced, would be harmful.

We know that guilt feelings are not always valid, and sometimes they can be self-destructive. We have seen that many common ways of handling guilt are unsound, either in theory or in practice. What, then, are the psychologically sound ways to handle guilt?

Learn the difference between realistic and unrealistic guilt. Many people carry a burden of guilt without reason. There are girls who, at any general accusation, are quick to feel ashamed. A teacher snaps, "This is the laziest class I've had in years," and such a girl, though she received an A from the same teacher, feels a wave of guilt.

The intensity of guilt feelings varies a great deal according to early training and experience. When you feel guilty, it is important to think out the reasons for it and to discern whether or not you're torturing yourself for an offense you didn't commit.

In judging your actions, take into account not only their effect but also their intent. If you accidentally drop a dozen eggs in the supermarket, you should feel far less guilty than if you had deliberately thrown them in a fit of anger at your younger brother.

Realistic guilt is a healthy reaction to a willful act (or omission) against your own code of behavior or a law of society. It should be handled differently from the way you deal with the unrealistic guilt you may feel from time to time.

Admit real guilt. Almost everybody has—in growing up—taken something that didn't belong to her, lied to a parent, revealed a friend's confidence, neglected a duty, been cruel to someone. Having done wrong, you feel "funny" about it. Admit that the funny feeling is guilt. Neither minimize nor exaggerate it; simply face it squarely. By honest acknowledgment of the fact that you have done wrong, you can begin to make reparations.

An eighteen-year-old girl was once referred to me by her family doctor after she had been in a series of accidents ranging from slight to near-fatal. I learned that these accidents had started shortly after she had stolen some money from the office of a summer camp where she had been a counselor. Just talking about her theft—she had not previously told anyone—relieved her feelings and helped her to understand that her accidents were an unconscious attempt to punish herself. It seemed, as she considered it reasonably, a poor kind of penance, doing no good to anybody. She decided, instead, to contact the camp director, confess her crime and offer to pay back what she had taken if he would allow it. The director was understanding and my patient took a part-time job in order to make her payments.

She continued therapy to get at the roots of her impulse to steal. But meantime, the accidents stopped. Her guilt, at least, had been handled soundly.

Profit from your mistakes. Once you have admitted your guilt and done something about it, stop beating yourself. Everyone makes mistakes; only the most arrogant person expects perfection of herself. To continue to berate yourself for a foolish or impulsive act that is over and done with is to indulge yourself in equally foolish and unproductive self-pity. If you have offended somebody, learn to be kinder. If you have spread malicious gossip, acknowledge your wrong and resolve not to repeat it. If you have disappointed a friend, determine to be a better friend in the future. If your guilt feelings awaken you to ways to improve yourself, they will be serving a good purpose.

Recognize the difference between thought and deed. Very few people would want to have their thoughts and feelings published. Almost everybody has ideas, daydreams and occasional fleeting thoughts that would be vicious or even criminal if translated into action.

There is a primitive element in all of us that, though buried under layers of civilization, still pops up in an occasional savage impulse. This part of us operates on the principle of immediate gratification. It says, "I want," and it is furious when denied its pleasures. The emotionally healthy person doesn't ignore or deny this instinct; she tries to tame it and to satisfy it within the context of her life and society.

The girl who isn't bearing an unrealistic sense of guilt can make a distinction between her thoughts and her actions. She holds herself responsible for her deeds and does not feel guilty about her thoughts.

You may be furious with your parents for making you baby-sit with your sister on the night of the sock hop. In your rage, you may imagine seeing her dead in her crib. There's no reason to feel guilty about it. But if you spend the evening badgering your sister and telling her scary stories, taking out your anger by making her miserable, then you should feel guilty. Perhaps your guilt feelings will help you to be a kinder sister.

Investigate your past. If guilt feelings persist no matter how carefully you avoid ruffling your conscience, it would be wise to consider why your conscience is such a bully. Some answers to the question are usually lying in a basket of childhood memories. Upbringing is a major factor in the building of a conscience; you will understand yours better when you think about your past.

Perhaps your parents expected and/or demanded great things of you and have left you with the habit of asking too much of yourself. If your parents were quick to punish and slow to forgive, maybe your conscience has taken over their role. Sometimes, in the heat of anger, a parent says things that are misunderstood by a small child. "You're making me sick!" is the kind of exaggeration that can echo in a child's mind and cause guilt feelings to grow there.

Little girls sometimes pull down their pants among a group of playmates. A parent who becomes overconcerned and punishes her child severely may leave her with a permanent sense of shame about her body.

A girl whose parents placed great emphasis on her being "ladylike" (which meant unaggressive) may grow up feeling guilty every time she asserts herself.

Even adults tend to feel a bit guilty when they do not act in accordance with the demands made upon them during childhood. Write down some of these demands and see if they don't help you understand yourself.

Accept responsibility for yourself. Some people seem to ride through life as if on horseback. Others seem to be the horses, driven this way and that by people and circumstance, never taking their own lead. By refusing responsibility, they can blame their mistakes on other people or on cruel fate. Follow-the-leader is an easy game to play, but it doesn't make a whole person. An adult who has achieved maturity holds herself accountable for her actions. Under orders or under influence, she takes the responsibility for what she does. Caught in a mistake, she doesn't blame it on somebody else. Even a third-grader knows that "But Billy made me do it" is not an acceptable excuse for having hit her playmate.

There is hardly anything in this world that anyone can force you to do if you really don't want to do it. Sometimes you may feel like an outcast or a killjoy, but if you remember that you are responsible for what you do, you won't let yourself be led into lowering your principles.

You may be surprised to find that when you speak up for your principles, others who were too timid to be the first will join you. When you begin to take full responsibility for yourself, you will learn the exhilarating fact that life is largely what you make it. It's responsibility that puts you in the driver's seat!

Make a smart investment. Many people feel guilty not because of something they've done but because of something they've failed to do. I'm not taking here about neglect of a duty, but there is a relationship between that and the neglect of an ability. When you have a talent, an aptitude or some potential ability which you are not using, you may feel guilty without knowing why. It seems as if human talents almost cry out to be used in a constructive way and if, for some reason, a person fails to use hers, the wasted energy turns into a kind of uneasiness that feels a lot like guilt.

Artists *should* paint. Dancers *should* dance. Athletes should use their bodies. "Brains" should use their minds. There is a lot of work to be done in the world and many ways for you to help do it. Use your abilities and you will reap the joy of achievement. A passive dropout from life helps nobody, least of all herself.

Work out your own standards. In our fast-moving world, it's hard to find an ethical code that will cover every situation. Absolute standards may have worked for people who stayed in small communities, dealing always with the same people and with recurrent situations. But in our fluid, changing society you can't predict from one day to the next whom you'll be dealing with and what you'll be dealing in. The trust you have in your parents and teachers might be folly if placed in a visiting sales manager who promises big profits *after* you've paid for the stationery kits he wants you to sell. The gentleness you strive for at home will perhaps be no asset when you're leading a rambunctious summer playground group. Friendliness to one boy is flirtation to another; honesty to one girl is insulting frankness to another. There is no set of rules you can count on invariably.

In a formal society like old Japan's, given questions have set responses and most situations proceed according to a commonly accepted ritual. Ours is a more casual society where on-the-spot judgment must often replace the ready-made answers of tradition-bound cultures. This relative freedom puts a lot of responsibility on the individual. It's up to you to set your own standards and to uphold them. The standards you set will be influenced by the demands of your one-of-a-kind conscience, but they should be arrived at with all the intelligence and sensibility you can muster.

A workable behavior code will include a great deal of your early discipline, the values of your family, your social background and your religious or ethical training. It will be influenced by what you have learned from your own experience and observation and, I hope, through reading and discussion. It will take into account the thinking of centuries of civilization as well as that of your contemporaries. It will come from both your mind and your heart.

Your principles, your own personal set of standards, will not, I'm afraid, prevent you from suffering guilt feelings, at least once in a while. But if your standards are sound and if you live by them, they will help to keep peace between you and your conscience.

Love and Sex

You are lucky to be growing up in a time when sex has emerged from its cover of shame and secrecy. Today's relative freedom, however, brings its own problems. While you no longer have to fight ignorance and taboos, you have choices and responsibilities your mothers and grandmothers didn't worry about because decisions were made for them and usually accepted without question.

The make-it-yourself decisions that you face boil down to your personal standards about your relationships with boys. These decisions should never be made lightly; yet help in making them is hard to come by. Many girls are reluctant to talk about sex with their parents, and many parents, unfortunately, are just as glad to be let off the hook. Just going along with your crowd—or with what you *think* your crowd is doing—means that you're not really coming to grips with *personal* standards. Talking things over with your girl friends can be a great relief: it's always helpful to know that other people share your problems. But you can't expect a girl your age to be a fountain of wisdom and information.

The fact is that most teen-agers talk a lot more sex than they actually practice. You should realize that a great deal of bravado and self-deceit—whistling in the dark—comes into play when one girl describes her experiences to another. Susie is much more likely to report a sexual adventure as "marvelous and exciting" than to admit that it was awkward and embarrassing and that she now feels guilty and humiliated. Similarly, the feelings of sex are expounded—and often exploited—in most of today's novels; but it would be a mistake to take lessons from them. Many novelists prefer to deal with the more sensational, eccentric and revolutionary aspects of people and experience. If you're planning to be sensational, eccentric or revolutionary, it's advisable to wait until you're mature enough to handle the great problems that almost inevitably accompany such behavior. There are, however, some helpful books written for young people which can give you insight and practical guidance to the world of male and female. I can recommend *Facts of Life and Love,* by Evelyn Millis Duvall,* and *How To Be a Successful Teen-ager,* by William Menninger, M.D.,† and *Love & Sex in Plain Language,* by Eric W. Johnson.‡

Certain questions about sex are asked repeatedly by teen-age girls. If you know the answers to them you will have a head start in working out your own individual solutions.

Are boys' feelings about sex different from girls'? Though it's not "sugar and spice and everything nice" as opposed to "snips and snails and puppy dogs' tails," there *is* a great biological and emotional difference between adolescent boys and girls. Sexual desire comes to boys in a great rush of emotion—an immediate, specific desire, quite separate from feelings of love. Development varies greatly, of course, but most boys are past voting age

*Associated Press, New York.
†Sterling Publishing Co., New York.
‡J. B. Lippincott, Philadelphia.

before they begin to experience a fusing of sexual drive and the deeper emotions of love and tenderness. A boy can be sincerely in love with one girl and at the same time be strongly physically attracted to another.

While there are some girls who can separate love from physical attraction, most of you will find your sexual desires closely bound to your thoughts and feelings of romantic love. Unlike a boy's, your mind and heart figuratively work together. Many girls don't experience frank sexual feelings until they are awakened in a powerful, romantic love relationship.

Boys, then, are able to—and likely to—be much more casual about sex than are girls. But though they are more casual before and after, they are also more urgent in the immediate moment of sexual encounter. Girls, with their over-all emotional involvement, tend to read deeper meanings into these encounters than boys do. Unless a girl understands this psychology, she is bound to be confused when a boy makes advances to her. It doesn't necessarily mean he loves her.

So it isn't an insult if a boy "makes a pass" at you; in a sense, that's his nature. But it is also not an insult to him if you refuse. Your own slower-rising, longer-lasting emotions are actually your protection against the consequences of allowing a boy's urgency to prevail—consequences which are much more serious to a girl than to a boy. For it isn't the boy who becomes pregnant or loses his good name, or even sits by the phone waiting for a call from a girl whose "line" he believed. As you grow older and wiser, you will be able to discriminate between the boy who really cares for you and the one who is simply expressing his maleness.

Among girls, even more than boys, sexual interest is highly individual: some girls at twelve are very much attracted to boys, and others—if they weren't pressured by their crowd—would be oblivious of the opposite sex until the late teens. There is no question of right and wrong when it comes to these feelings; it is rather a question of physical and psychological make-up. The rights and wrongs pertain to what you *do* with these feelings or nonfeelings.

Does a contract for a date include a good-night kiss clause? Some girls feel guilty if they don't kiss a boy on their first date. Others feel guilty if they do. There are all kinds of kisses, and there is nothing wrong with a light good-night kiss if you like the boy, had a good time and would like him to know it. But a kiss is a token of affection and it would be silly—not to say insincere —to kiss a boy just to pay him off for taking you out. There is nothing wrong, either, with a squeeze of the hand and a warm "thank you" after the most delightful date. Kissing good night is a case of "doing what comes naturally." Most girls don't really feel like getting too close too quickly. If you follow these feelings, you probably won't find yourself in uncomfortably close situations with boys you don't know well. But if you do let a good-night kiss become a big production, don't blame the boy for thinking you're fast.

What's the difference between necking and petting? Necking is often defined as physical contact between a boy and girl above his necktie and her string of pearls. Actually, it is more a question of intensity than geography. Necking is light sex play. In our culture, it can be very casual, beginning with party games like spin-the-bottle and going on to less formalized kissing in more private surroundings.

Petting is the intense physical contact that creates and propels sexual excitement. In the great scheme of things, petting is activity really designed to prepare a couple for sexual intercourse. Certain parts of our bodies are particularly sensitive to sexual stimulation; again, the sensitivity varies greatly from person to person. Petting includes physical exploration and excitation between a boy and a girl, short of actual sexual intercourse. Enormous physical and emotional pressures are unleashed. It is during petting sessions that many boys and girls find their temperatures rising higher than their IQs—and their judgment gets drowned in a flood of feeling.

Petting therefore can be dangerous because it accelerates passion, invites loss of control. Sadly, some girls make a game of petting and pride themselves on being able to "shut it off." This attitude, for one thing, is unfair to the boy, who may feel, with justification, that he has been teased or taken advantage of. Some psychologists believe that this sudden shutting off of passion leaves both boy and girl with unhealthy tensions and frustrations and may even deter sexual compatibility later on in grownup sexual relationships. But primarily, we need only think about the growing number of premature marriages, illegal abortions and children born out of wedlock to realize that the "shutting off" technique is often too little and too late. As petting experiments become more daring—and very few people don't advance with time and intimacy—that danger threshold comes even closer. You might go through it.

Can I maintain my standards and *my popularity?* Popularity is based more on personality and companionship than on sexual activity. A girl who necks or pets in order to get or keep dates is putting herself in the position of being paid for services rendered. A buy-and-sell arrangement isn't really popularity. True, young men will compete to see who can get the furthest with Sue, but after a flurry of dates, Sue is usually dropped while the contest moves along to some other girl.

There probably will be some boys who won't take no for an answer—that is, who won't come back after your refusal to neck or pet, or play the game their way. But these conquering types don't stay around long in any case. Even if you say yes, they'll soon be looking for new fields to conquer. By that time you, with your more complex emotions, will be tied in knots, but they will have no ties to bind them. This is the very old, common heartbreak story—the girl who falls for a "line," gives in and then is devastated to learn that the boy is no longer interested. "Love 'em and leave 'em" is seldom a girl's slogan. But seventy percent of college-educated men have sexual intercourse before marriage and only seventeen percent limit it to their fiancées.

How does a girl set standards? Your own personal standards should be decided upon only after long, serious consideration of your emotional make-up, your religious feelings, your relationship with the boy in question, the society you live in and your concept of who you are and what you want in life. A large order? Yes! The kind of straight thinking and deep thinking most seventeen-year-olds are up to? No! And a split-second decision in the back seat of an automobile almost always calls up the wrong answer.

Things were, in a way, simpler fifty years ago, when girls weren't expected to enjoy sex. Indeed, they were taught that sex was to be tolerated, a biological duty of marriage. Today, almost everyone—including most parents—regards sex as a normal part of life. Along with your appetite for food and learning, you have a healthy appetite for the fulfillment of love.

With freedom to choose your own escorts and to spend time alone with them, it's clear that how far you go sexually is up to you. There are few boys who won't go as far as a girl will let them, and who will not try to go a step further than that—and I'm talking about "nice" boys, the kind you bring home to Mother. The sensible, mature girl will use her sexual freedom wisely—in its proper time, place and social context. She will let it enrich a relationship that is solid and deeply meaningful and permanent. She will not use it as a toy or a tool or a weapon.

Available statistical sources estimate that from 1940 to 1960, the percent of live births that were illegitimate increased from 3.8 to 5.3 in the thirty-three states reporting. There are now 250,000 illegitimate births a year and a soaring rate of illegal abortions. The fact that a woman is unmarried is not grounds for legal abortion in this country; illegal abortion is expensive, sometimes physically dangerous and almost always psychologically devastating. Of the marriages of necessity, one in three ends in early divorce.

Among the unmarried teen-agers I talk to, almost all who have lost their virginity regret it afterward. Often these girls come to realize that their action was based on feelings other than love: it is more often a form of rebellion against parental authority or a desperate search for security than a response to normal sexual appetites. The "fast" girl, then, is almost always someone who is using sex to work out problems that have little to do with sex; and her "solution" only creates deeper problems. As a "revenge" against parents, it's a case of cutting off one's nose to spite one's face. And as for security, hardly anything is less secure than a teen-age "affair."

How do I call a halt? In our society, it's the girl who has ultimate control. I've never met a girl who was seduced without somehow having "asked for it." Boys are expected to try. They try without necessarily expecting anything to happen—but they try because they think this is the role they must play. When a girl honestly and tactfully refuses, the boy is not really hurt or angry—and sometimes he is actually relieved to be reassured that "she's really a nice girl."

You may think this is an unfair and even hypocritical way for boys to behave. Yet it is a fact that most boys lose respect for an "easy mark," and after a torrid affair, are quite likely to decide that the young woman is "not the kind of girl I want to be the mother of my children." Despite all talk to the contrary, our society is still caught up in the "double standard," by which a young man expects to have premarital sexual contacts and, at the same time, prefers to marry a virgin.

You may decide at some point that you don't believe in the double standard, that you wouldn't want to marry a man who did. My advice is to wait to make that decision until you're out of your teens. Such a decision calls for more maturity than a teen-ager can muster; adolescence is a period when emotions and mentality are working overtime to catch up with physical develop-ment—you simply don't have the balance or the life experience to meet the problems that such a decision opens up. As for now, the only way you can protect yourself from the hurts caused by double-standard behavior is to call that halt before you've lost your "good girl" status.

An ounce of prevention is worth a pound of halt-calling. If you *keep* yourself out of hot situations, you won't have to *get* yourself out of them. Make it plain that you *don't* want to leave the party early, that you *don't* want to park by the lake, that you *don't* want to spend an evening alone together in his house or your house while your parents are out. Likewise, *don't* invite trouble by looking and acting cheap. If you call attention to yourself with overdone hairdos and make-up, with too-tight sweaters and too-loose walk, you shouldn't be surprised at getting asked to lonely strolls in the woods or drives to lovers' lane. If you really aren't about to offer the product, then don't advertise.

Sometimes, despite your precautions, you may find yourself in a situation where you *must* call a halt. An honest explanation of your feelings will never break off a relationship with any man who is worth caring about. If he is interested only in your body, it's better to know now than later.

Older girls who are engaged or who have been going steady for a long time have a different kind of problem. Perhaps they have been dating the same boy for two years, are sincerely in love and planning to marry. Gradually their intimacy has increased from light necking to heavy petting until now they don't see how they can possibly keep from going further.

The situation calls for a serious appraisal of the physical dangers involved in premarital intercourse. There is always the danger of pregnancy. No contraceptive yet invented is one hundred percent safe in actual practice. There is also a chance of contracting a venereal disease. Syphilis and gonorrhea, both transmitted through sexual intercourse, have reached epidemic proportions, their occurrence having almost doubled in the United States in the past eight years. Among teen-agers, reported cases of new syphilis increased more than two hundred percent between 1956 and 1963. Both these venereal diseases are difficult to detect in the early stages and devastating if left untreated. In addition, sexual contact is occasionally followed by various less serious infections and complications which call for a bit of medical attention.

Let's take a straight look at the psychological dangers, too. Thanks to hazily romantic books and movies and sometimes to reports from girls who hope to justify their behavior or to entice others into imitating it (misery loves company?), many of you believe your first experience will be accompanied by the ringing of bells and the trilling of bluebirds. Actually, sexual compatibility frequently takes quite a while to achieve. For many women, it takes many months to reach full sexual satisfaction, this in the most secure of marital relationships. A girl with the added problems of fearing pregnancy, wondering if anybody will find out, worrying that her fiancé will change his mind about marrying her—and feeling guilty about the whole thing—is not likely to get or give full enjoyment in sex.

Her fears are well based. Some studies show that twice as many engagements are broken among couples who have had intercourse; the more frequent the intercourse, the greater the number of marriages canceled. There is no doubt that many a man's desire for marriage decreases when his girl friend sleeps with him. For most girls, alas, the opposite is true. Furthermore, couples who have intercourse before marriage are more likely to be divorced or separated or to indulge in adultery than others. One way or another, premarital intimacy is more closely related to broken relationships than to solid ties.

If after considering these points a girl decides that it simply isn't worth the risks, then she must explain her feelings to her young man and ask for his cooperation. He may put up a fuss, but a man will take into account the convictions of the girl he loves.

What is called for, in such a situation, is a change of courting patterns: more time spent with other people, time with your parents and his, with friends, plenty of activities. Arrange parties, take up bowling, tennis or horseback riding. Participating in active sports together can provide a great release of sexual energy. A boy who says, "If you really loved me, you would," can be truthfully answered: "If you really loved me, you wouldn't insist."

I got into trouble once. What can I do now? If there is a girl reading these words now who feels that her life is ruined because of some mistake she has made, let her be assured that what she does today and tomorrow is far more important than what she did in the past.

When you have violated your personal standards or those of society, it's natural to suffer some pangs of guilt. The important thing is not to allow yourself the luxury of wallowing in self-pity, a mortification that does nobody any good and certainly doesn't undo your mistake. If you really feel that you cannot rejoin the stream of life, get some help from your religious adviser, a qualified psychologist or other professional counselor. The people who love you probably forgive you, but you must learn to forgive yourself.

No experience in life is ever wasted or wholly bad if we learn from it. Our mistakes can help us grow and often to become better people.

A girl needs both inner strength and outside help in getting through a premarital pregnancy. But there are other, more common kinds of trouble. Some boys do seduce girls and then let the whole town know about it. Sometimes a thoughtless act in a careless moment can make a girl the subject of widespread gossip. But more often than not, your feeling that "everybody knows what happened" is more a reflection of your own guilt and desire for punishment than of actual public disapproval. Most people are much too occupied with their own immediate problems and interests to spend hours devising ways to embarrass you and exclude you because of something you've done. And even if you *are* the subject of gossip, try to remember that gossipers seek ever-new subject matter and they will soon move on to other targets. Until it blows over, you would be wise to hold up your head, keep up with your usual activities and remember that you're as good as you are today and will be even better tomorrow. Now you will know enough to avoid the people and situations that got you into trouble in the first place.

If you are in serious trouble right now and don't know what to do, here's what *not* to do. Don't panic and don't discuss your problems with classmates or neighbors. See someone who can really help. If you feel you can't go to your parents, talk to the school psychologist, the family doctor, your clergyman or even a trusted teacher—but talk to an adult who can be objective as well as sympathetic. They've probably heard the story before and can help to put you on the right track. *Nobody is really alone unless she chooses to be.*

I thought it was love, but now I've changed my mind. What can I do? A girl who has had intercourse with a boy because she thought she was in love with him often finds herself in this predicament. The emotional ties are strong. She may feel she has to marry him to preserve her honor. She may feel she is not in a position to start dating other boys now that she "belongs" to her lover. She may think that, as a "secondhand" commodity, her chances for winning another husband are diminished. But time and experience have opened her eyes: her boy friend is *not* the man she now wants to spend her life with. Physical attraction and immaturity blinded her to characteristics that she now knows would produce an unhappy marriage. Can she turn her back on this deep involvement?

Of course she can. And she'd better do it fast. Habit, loyalty, insecurity and a shared guilt do not make the kind of relationship that should continue into marriage. The sooner a girl gets out of it, the better for both girl and boy. If it's hard to do it now, it will be harder next month and still harder in half a year. Again, an honest confrontation with your own feelings should lead to an honest confrontation with the young man. Hurt him now and hurt yourself now, if you must, for you'll be saving both of you from the greater hurt of an unhappy marriage.

As for the fact that you have lost your virginity, there is no need for it to be mentioned. Forget the past; it is today and tomorrow which matter far more. When you think seriously about marrying the man you really love, you might want to tell him about your one affair and, in all probability, he will love you enough to overlook it.

What's the matter with me? I don't feel a thing. You may wonder what all the shouting is about. Here you are in your midteens and you never have to control your feelings because you don't seem to have any. You've heard about "frigid" women and you're beginning to think you're one of them. What's going to happen when you get married?

Sex is, as I've said before, a highly individual matter and there is no "proper" amount of feeling. We all have different sexual responses, just as we all have different IQs and different talents. Men, too, have varying degrees of sexuality; through our free-choice system of dating and mating, we do tend to team up with our match.

There could be many reasons for your seeming detachment. They could be purely physical, due to the workings of your sex glands. They could be psychological, due to early experiences or to fears about the dangers of sex. Or the reason could be simply that you haven't yet found the man to whom you can naturally respond. There is no standard that you have to come up to. The girl who feels no desire at all is not necessarily less normal than the girl who is continually bothered by sexual thoughts or the girl with very casual sex interest.

If you are deeply troubled, however, by any problem that makes you feel "different," it would be wise to talk it over with an expert. If it's nothing to worry about, you might as well get the good word from an authority. And if you have a real problem, it's better to work it out than to worry about it.

A word in conclusion. Sex can be compared to atomic energy. It is a powerful force. Used wisely, it can warm our lives and enrich a meaningful relationship. Used carelessly or wantonly, it can cause an emotional explosion that may blow up our chances for happiness. Most of us believe that sexual as well as atomic energy should be used for constructive purposes.

How To Handle a Crisis

Though we optimistic Americans like to sing that "everything's coming up roses," the truth is that not every cloud has a silver lining. All of you will encounter sorrowful or distressing experiences and few will grow up without suffering deep hurt or shock, losses, disappointments, failures and at least an occasional problem that seems to have no solution.

Sometimes, too, a fairly superficial shock can shatter your sense of well-being and hurl you into despair. A near-miss car accident or a quarrel with a classmate may leave you upset for days. A fire in your neighbor's garage, theft in your school or dormitory, the loss of a prize you expected to win or a boy friend you wanted to keep may suddenly turn your world from a comfortable, predictable place into a frightening jungle. Your reaction to these situations will depend on your current state of mind as well as your general attitude toward trouble. A girl who expects nothing but the best can be unsettled by a fairly trivial disappointment that might be shrugged off by a more stoical friend. A girl who has had more than her quota of recent frustrations may go to pieces on hearing a bit of bad news that would not ordinarily upset her.

And there are times when even the most philosophical and successful of us is severely shaken. To recognize the possibilities of loss and pain is one thing; to face them is quite another. Real trouble—serious illness or death in the family, debilitation of a parent, loss of financial security or family breakup—can arise at any time.

Your problem may be specific or general: rejection by a college, a chronic poor relationship with a parent, a breakup with
a boy friend, gossip about you or your own suspicion that you're
ill. When you are terribly upset—whether the trouble is great
or small, whether it's real or imagined—there *is* something that
you can do about it. I am not saying that you can come out of
every crisis unscathed or unscarred. But there are some sound
psychological principles that will help you to handle your problem and to regain your equilibrium.

1. *Face it.* Living in a turmoil of anxious speculation is harder
than living with cold facts. Moreover, you cannot begin to act
upon a problem until you know exactly what it is. If you're
afraid you're failing in chemistry, talk to your chemistry teacher,
learn where you stand, and if you really are standing in a ditch,
get some help to pull yourself out. If you suspect there is something physically wrong with you, a medical checkup will either
prove that you're wrong or set you on the road to proper treatment. Shutting your eyes to trouble won't make the trouble
disappear.

2. *Put it on paper.* When a situation begins to go out of control
many girls find they can rein it in by writing it down. Unwieldy
abstractions become less troublesome when they are set down
tangibly in black and white. Orderly lists seem to tame disorderly
thoughts. If you are struggling with difficult alternatives, a listing
of the merits and drawbacks of each choice may help you to
make the wiser one. Bowed by a deep disappointment, you may

be cheered by listing some of the good things that have happened to you recently and some more good things that you might enjoy in the near future.

3. *Take one step at a time.* "I don't know what to do first" is the way many people describe their feelings during a crisis. Faced with a serious problem, you, too, may feel like the man who jumped on his horse and rode off in all directions. Most people, however, can do well only one thing at a time. So no matter how overwhelming the tasks before you seem to be, the place to start is at the beginning and the way to proceed is one step at a time. Even if you cannot see a clear beginning, it's important to start *somewhere,* anywhere. If you don't know where to start, pick up the quickest or easiest job—no matter how trivial —then the next. Once you get into the swing of accomplishment, the harder jobs will probably fall into line.

4. *But take the steps.* Worry travels in circles that can become wider and wider until they envelop you. Whether you are assaulted by doubts or stunned by shocking news, you are better off moving than sitting still. Oppressed by a feeling that your fiancé is acting distant lately, you won't help the situation by catching yourself in a web of frantic wondering. Tell him how you feel and why, and you may learn either that you're wrong or what *is* wrong. If there's something wrong, perhaps you can improve it; if your fiancé really does want to break up, then best get it done with, for no amount of worrying will help.

When there is a death in the family or of someone else very

close, there is bound to be a deep feeling of loss. At first the mind may refuse to accept the dreadful reality of death; one cries out, "Oh, no!" One may feel only numb or stunned for a period of hours or even days. When the initial shock has been absorbed, however, the usual reaction is grief and depression and perhaps the feeling that nothing will ever be right again. It is, of course, normal to mourn the death of a loved one and most psychologists agree that grief should be outwardly expressed. Everyone has her own ways of expressing emotions, but, in general, weeping and "talking it out" are healthy ways to express grief. They help decrease the more pathological reactions when grief turns inward: loss of appetite, sleeplessness, protracted depression. Nobody can predict the duration of a mourning period and perhaps the wisest thing to do is to let it run its course. Remember that time is the great healer. Even when the acute grief has subsided, much more time may be required for a complete recovery of spirit. And still later, there may be recurrences of grief—at certain memories or anniversaries. If several months do not bring about a *lessening* of grief, the mourner should consider the possibility of seeking some professional assistance.

5. *Put personal problems under your pillow.* "Sleep on it" is old-fashioned advice to people juggling important decisions. But it's also as modern as the science of psychology. Recent studies have proved what most people have known for a long time, that sleep—as Shakespeare put it—"knits up the ravell'd sleeve of care." Fatigue is the enemy of clear thought. When you are tired,

your judgment apparatus does not function as well as when you are well rested. If you feel assaulted by a tremendous problem—a decision on which your future seems to hang, a situation that seems unbearable, a mood of terrible anxiety or doubt—try to get a good night's sleep (or at least a good rest) before you act on it.

6. *Don't be a blame-thrower.* When trouble strikes, there is a tendency to look for someone to blame it on. Many of us, when hurt or shocked, seem to want to inflict punishment for the pain that we suffer. But fault-finding in times of distress seldom helps anybody and often does a great deal of unnecessary harm.

Meg's mother came down with a high fever and, in the heat of suspense while the doctor was examining her, Meg turned on her brother. "It's all your fault!" she accused him. "You made her go out in the rain last night to put your bike away!" The scolding didn't help Meg's mother, and it didn't help Meg's brother who felt as worried as Meg. And all it did for Meg was to add guilt to her concern for her mother.

It is unfortunate when, after an emergency has cleared up, we are left with a residue of grudges and regrets due to thoughtless blame-throwing under pressure.

7. *Don't victimize yourself.* "If only I hadn't . . ." and "I should have . . ." and "This wouldn't have happened if I'd . . ." are very frequent reactions to disasters that were really unavoidable or completely accidental. Self-blame is another destructive reaction. Whether or not you could have prevented the trouble

is not so important as what you are doing now to alleviate it. But if you permit yourself to drown in a deluge of guilt, you won't be much help to those on shore.

None of us is blameless but, particularly during crises, we should be charitable to ourselves. When Sally's father died of a heart attack, Sally began to berate herself for having been a bad daughter. She thought of all the things that she might have done to please him and had left undone. She recalled bitterly every incident of rudeness or disobedience, every disagreement and every annoyance she had caused him. Perhaps if she had shoveled the snow last month—she told herself—this wouldn't have happened. If she had been less extravagant—she mourned—he might have had fewer financial worries. Why hadn't she spent more evenings at home with the family? Why had she dropped piano lessons when he had so greatly enjoyed her playing?

If Sally had been able to see herself objectively, she would have understood that she was neither more nor less than a normal daughter. She would have seen that she was condemning herself unfairly and that her excessive guilt was an unhealthy way to cope with her grief.

8. *What do you really want?* When you are overwhelmed with an emotional problem, it is important to know why. If the causes of your upset are clear to you, then your job is to cope with them as effectively as possible. But sometimes you may find yourself troubled out of all proportion to the obvious causes. In such cases there is always a reason for your feelings: people

do not suffer scarlet fever symptoms if the only thing wrong with them is a common cold. If you are deeply depressed, unnaturally irritable, restless or agitated, *something* is wrong even if that something is not immediately evident.

One fairly dependable way to get to the root of your malaise is to figure out what it is you want from life and are not getting. If you allow yourself the time and honesty to search for your true feelings, you may find that you have simply taken a wrong turn somewhere along the road or that your foot is on the gas pedal and the brake at the same time.

Instead of being joyous about her wedding plans, Jill became increasingly apprehensive and indecisive. She was unable to choose a wedding date, to select a gown, to make up a guest list. For a while she attributed her confusion to premarriage jitters; but when her fiancé and her parents tried to speed things up, Jill went into a panic that could not be so lightly disclaimed.

Her parents wisely cut off all wedding talk and suggested that Jill take some time to think things over. Jill went to visit an aunt, at whose quiet house she could retreat from all the pressures of her social life. There she was finally forced to face the fact that she really did not want to marry her fiancé, no matter how good a "catch" he was. It wasn't easy to break her engagement, return her gifts and get back into circulation; but once she had uncovered her real feelings, she saw very clearly that it was the only right thing to do. Having made her decision, Jill was able again to function efficiently.

When you find that you are unable to make a decision, chances are that the reason lies in your not knowing what you really want or not being able to relinquish what you really can't keep.

9. *There are many paths through the forest.* Great disappointments occasionally derail a teen-ager and sometimes it's very difficult to get back on the track. When a carefully constructed project fails to work out or a cherished dream is suddenly exploded, you may feel that life has lost all joy and meaning.

At such times it's helpful to remember that there is more than one way to get through a forest. If one goal proves to be unattainable, perhaps there are other worthwhile ends—often closely related—that you can achieve. You can spend a lifetime regretting your lost cause or pursuing a hopeless dream. But you'll have a better life if you find an alternative that can give you at least partial satisfaction and at best—because it's attainable—complete fulfillment.

From her kindergarten days, Rae wanted to be a nurse. Her back porch was a hospital for wounded birds. Neighborhood children came to her to have splinters removed and cuts bandaged. Asked what she wanted for birthday gifts as a child, her choices were always in the line of first-aid equipment and nurses' uniforms. It was generally accepted that, with her gentle and sympathetic disposition, she'd make a wonderful nurse. What nobody—especially Rae—had expected was that she would not be accepted in a nursing school.

Her dream fell apart gradually, all during her senior year in high school, as one rejection after another arrived until it was clear that she was not going to make it. Rae knew, of course, that her marks were poor, but until the last school refused her, she had kept hoping to squeeze by. She was lost and miserable; she had never thought of any future other than nursing and, without nursing school, there was nothing to look forward to.

Fortunately, there was a guidance counselor who had been trying to help Rae find a school that would accept her. Rae returned to the counselor and was flexible enough to take his advice and enroll in a practical nursing course. She will not be an R.N., but she will become a practical nurse and find plenty of satisfying work to do in the field of her original choice.

10. *Not everything can be made better.* Many problem situations turn out well. Even serious trouble can often be looked back on as opportunity for growth and improved understanding. Many evils can be seen as challenges to show what we can do to improve them. But there are some problems that cannot be solved felicitously, some victims who do not live happily ever after and some situations that absolutely no good can arise from. The dead cannot be returned to life; a dead relationship cannot be fanned into a new flame. We can apologize for an act of foolishness or cruelty, but we cannot erase it. Some situations are beyond our control; we can do nothing to change them. There are times when we are simply not in the saddle and all we can do is watch the horses run wild. The mature human being recognizes the fact that she is not all-powerful. Up against a

situation that cannot be changed, she accepts it and turns her energies to more fruitful matters.

A large number of organizations that raise funds to help medical research were founded in memory of victims of specific diseases, for the purpose of fighting that disease. This, like the practice of sending individual charity contributions in memory of the dead, is an example of accepting the inevitable and turning to the improvable.

11. *When, where, how to get outside help.* Some girls prefer to wrestle alone with their problems while others find comfort in talking about them. As we know, talking about troubles is a good way to discharge tension and sometimes to clarify your thinking. But it's wise to be selective about your audience. You might not enjoy hearing one of your confidences shared at a twirlers' club meeting, nor would you care to have it brought up against you in future quarrels.

If you are going through a period of insecurity and self-doubt, it's often bracing to mull things over with a good, sympathetic friend, who has probably felt the same way at one time or another. But if you have a specific, serious problem, you cannot expect that friend—no more experienced or expert than you— to give you the kind of help you may need. When your problems get out of control, when you are deeply disturbed and unable to cope with your troubles by yourself, there are several outside resources to which you can turn for help.

Your parents can almost always be counted on. Despite day-to-day friction in many families, most parents really do care and will stand up for you when you need them. Their point of view is seasoned by years of living, and when you're in real trouble, your parents are your natural first resource. Many girls have found unsuspected depths of understanding when they have gone in distress to parents who ordinarily kept a polite distance or seemed not to take their daughters seriously.

If, however, you find it impossible to communicate with your parents, or if you feel that your problem exists *because* of your parents, seek competent adult help elsewhere.

Guidance counselors who specialize in vocational, social and personal areas are employed by most high schools.

Part of their job is to be informed about community agencies that can help students in distress. Of course, guidance counselors are not infallible and you probably know from classmates if the one in your school is indifferent or ineffectual.

If there are no guidance services in your school and you feel that you need aptitude testing, write to the American Personnel and Guidance Association, 1534 O Street, N.W., Washington, D.C. 20005, for a directory of qualified guidance agencies.

Psychologists have joined the staffs of increasing numbers of school systems, specifically to help students with emotional problems. A psychologist usually has a Ph.D. and is a specialist in understanding and evaluating human behavior. School psychologists have at hand a number of tests that can help you to define your areas of strength and weakness. They can usually be relied upon to possess the insight and objectivity—and the experience with people your age—to understand your state of mind. When you have a problem that doesn't yield to your own efforts for solution, feel free to make an appointment with your school psychologist. He's there to help you.

If your school does not offer psychological services, you can obtain a list of qualified psychologists and psychological clinics in your community by writing to or telephoning the psychology department of the college nearest you.

You should be able to trust your doctor to keep your confidences as well as to guard your health. If you cannot, perhaps you should find another doctor. Many emotional problems derive from physical problems: jitters and irritability or lack of energy might well be symptoms of malnutrition. A simple blood test can indicate, for example, a low blood sugar content or a vitamin deficiency. A number of viruses cause weakness and depression without easily detectable physical symptoms.

Since early detection and treatment offer the best promise of cure for many disorders, there is no good reason to delay seeing a doctor. Some girls hesitate because they are embarrassed about the nature of their complaint or overmodest about physical examination. To a doctor, however, the human body is an impersonal object and there is probably nothing about it that he hasn't seen or diagnosed many times before. If you cannot overcome your reluctance, you might find it easier to go to a woman doctor.

Problems completely apart from the physical—unhappy relationships, frustrations, difficult choices—are not beyond the scope of a doctor in whom you feel confidence. In addition to knowing a great deal about people's bodies, most physicians—after a few years in practice—know a great deal about their feelings. There is very little you could tell your doctor that he hasn't heard before. And, because he hears so much about human troubles, he may be in a singularly good position to alleviate yours. In rare cases, when the ability to function in society is severely impaired by emotional disturbance, a physician may recommend the services of a psychiatrist, who is a medical doctor specializing in emotional illness.

If you are looking for a doctor, you can get the names of qualified physicians from your county medical society.

Your clergyman is more than a prayer leader and a director of religious ritual. Most modern ministers, priests and rabbis not only are students of human nature but also have had training in psychology and counseling. If your problem has moral or ethical aspects, a clergyman is an obvious source of help. Even if your distress seems to be outside his sphere of operation and even if you are not a regular churchgoer, a talk with a clergyman whom you respect may help you get a long-range view of what's bothering you: much of the collected wisdom that forms the basis of religions is practical psychology relevant to modern situations.

The YWCA, the YWHA, youth centers, settlement houses often

employ professional youth workers who are trained to understand the problems of girls your age. Such an adviser may be able to help you directly or to refer you to a social service agency that can.

The Y itself has ways of helping to resolve many social problems: an adviser may suggest a club in which a girl can make new friends; classes (in cooking, sewing, dancing) where she can find satisfaction in developing new skills; or a sports and exercise program to help solve a figure problem. Furthermore, there are volunteer service groups where one can find release from her troubles by helping others.

Community services vary widely, but your local health officer will know the ones available to meet your needs. In many areas there are housekeeping services that lend a hand when there is illness in the family; visiting nurses; family counselors and welfare offices. Alcoholics Anonymous has coast-to-coast chapters, listed in the telephone book, with a branch called Alateen to help the teen-age children of alcoholics. Mental health clinics are operating in more and more communities. For the address of the one nearest you, ask your local health officer or write to American Mental Health Foundation, Inc., 2 East 86th Street, New York, New York 10028, or the National Association for Mental Health, Inc., 10 Columbus Circle, New York, New York 10019.

The library is a vast and easily available source of insight into human problems. If you have read widely, you have probably already discovered factual and fictional girls who have faced troubles similar to yours. Reading an honest, intelligent novel about somebody like you can be both illuminating and comforting. An English teacher or librarian who knows you well might be able to make good suggestions.

There are also innumerable nonfiction books dealing with specific areas in which your troubles may lie: books on colleges and how to apply for admission; books on careers; books about sex and dating, etiquette and self-improvement; books about fashion and budgeting, about philosophy and religion; books about teen-age problems. Two of the latter that I particularly recommend are *The Art of Growing,* by Robert Nixon,* and *Love, Sex and the Teen-ager,* by Rhoda Lorand.†

Public Affairs Pamphlets, a nonprofit educational organization, distributes hundreds of excellent, timely pamphlets with titles ranging from "Young Adults and Their Parents" to "If I Marry Outside My Religion" to "Foodlore for Teen-Agers." For a catalog, write to 381 Park Avenue South, New York, New York 10016.

Books, people and agencies can help to give you insight into your problems and to put you in the right direction toward solving or learning to live with them. But books and advisers alone cannot do the whole job. Your own understanding and strength and will to overcome your difficulties are essential agents. Never hesitate to look for help in coping with a crisis. But never forget to help those who are trying to help you.

*Random House, New York.
†Macmillan, New York.